"Bree Picower continues to lead in anti-racist teacher education. *Reading, Writing, and Racism* is eminently useful for pre-service and in-service teachers to reflect on how they may have perpetuated whiteness in their own teaching or experienced it as students themselves. This is a must-read for all future and current teachers interested in racial justice in the classroom."

—WAYNE AU,
editor of Rethinking Schools

"*Reading, Writing, and Racism* is a critical and urgently needed text. Bree Picower brilliantly analyzes the long-standing and constitutive relationship between American schooling, curriculum, and structural racism. With strong theory, critical analysis, and actionable examples, Picower creates space to reimagine school as a site of anti-racist praxis. This book is essential reading for teachers, parents, and everyday citizens looking to dismantle White supremacy and expand justice."

—MARC LAMONT HILL,
author of Nobody: Casualties of America's War on
the Vulnerable, from Ferguson to Flint and Beyond

"The egregious, racist actions of a subset of school teachers that have gone viral on social media may seem like outliers in an otherwise just system and profession, but they are not, as argued compellingly in *Reading, Writing, and Racism*. What and how we teach, and who teaches, and how we prepare them should not be presumed to be somehow immune from the long legacies of white supremacy and colonialism that have shaped US schooling from its very beginning. Reframing and reorienting more forcefully toward racial justice requires tackling these legacies head-on in programs that prepare, support, connect, celebrate, and hold accountable educators—and Bree Picower offers us frameworks, models, and hope for doing precisely that, when the need could not be more great."

—KEVIN KUMASHIRO,
author of Bad Teacher! How Blaming
Teachers Distorts the Bigger Picture

"*Reading, Writing, and Racism* places the emphasis on interrupting racism in teacher preparation programs and schools where it belongs—not simply on individual beliefs and actions but on primarily broader policies and practices that continue to maintain and protect racist ideology. Based on years of research and chockful of curriculum examples—both horrific and positive—and using case studies of actual anti-racist teacher education pro-grams around the nation, Bree Picower's book describes the myriad ways in which these programs address racism and center social justice. With power-ful insights and concrete suggestions for transformation, *Reading, Writing, and Racism* is certain to help teachers, teacher educators, and administra-tors rethink their roles in preparing the nation's teachers."

—SONIA NIETO,
professor emerita, Language, Culture, and Teaching,
University of Massachusetts, Amherst, and author of
Brooklyn Dreams: My Life in Public Education

"Coupling an urgent call to action with the practical supports required to act, this book offers a vision for and examples of the kind of humanizing, healing practices that successfully prepare teachers to struggle for racial justice through their everyday work. For those committed to rooting out the curricular violence of Whiteness, this book is right on time."

—CARLA SHALABY,
author of Troublemakers: Lessons in
Freedom from Young Children at School

"*Reading, Writing, and Racism* is a clearly written, no-holds-barred gem of a book that every teacher educator must read. Drawing on her incisive cri-tique of curriculum and teacher ideology, along with interviews with racial justice teacher educators, Picower cogently frames how whiteness works in teacher education, while showing us how to upend it."

—CHRISTINE SLEETER,
coauthor of Transformative Ethnic Studies in
Schools: Curriculum, Pedagogy, and Research

"In concert with the current moment of racial reckoning, the contributions of Dr. Bree Picower push us to acknowledge and remember the totalizing power of white supremacy in curriculum. Her bravery, humility, and criti-cality offer strength for folks who dare to do revolutionary classroom work when the world feels like it's upside-down. If you consider yourself an ally in the struggle for racial justice, you cannot turn away from this book!"

—DAVID STOVALL,
author of Born Out of Struggle: Critical Race Theory,
School Creation, and the Politics of Interruption

READING, WRITING, AND RACISM

READING, WRITING, AND RACISM

**DISRUPTING WHITENESS
IN TEACHER EDUCATION
AND IN THE CLASSROOM**

BREE PICOWER

FOREWORD BY BETTINA L. LOVE

BEACON PRESS, BOSTON

BEACON PRESS
Boston, Massachusetts
www.beacon.org

Beacon Press books
are published under the auspices of
the Unitarian Universalist Association of Congregations.

24 23 22 21   8 7 6 5 4 3 2 1

This book is printed on acid-free paper that meets the uncoated paper
ANSI/NISO specifications for permanence as revised in 1992.

Text design by Wilsted & Taylor Publishing Services

Library of Congress Cataloging-in-Publication Data

Names: Picower, Bree, author.
Title: Reading, writing, and racism : disrupting whiteness in teacher education
and in the classroom / Bree Picower.
Description: Boston, Massachusetts : Beacon Press, 2021. | Includes
bibliographical references and index.
Identifiers: LCCN 2020022060 (print) | LCCN 2020022061 (ebook) | ISBN
9780807033708 (hardcover) | ISBN 9780807033715 (ebook)
Subjects: LCSH: Racism in education—United States. | Discrimination in
education—United States. | Teachers—Training of—Social
aspects—United States.
Classification: LCC LC212.2 .P53 2021 (print) | LCC LC212.2
(ebook) | DDC
371.829/00973—dc23
LC record available at https://lccn.loc.gov/2020022060
LC ebook record available at https://lccn.loc.gov/2020022061

This book is dedicated to Antonio Nieves Martinez, a member of our educational justice family whose life binds us together and whose spirit guides our collective work to center love and liberation within education.

100 percent of the royalties of this book will be donated to two grassroots organizations led by people of Color dedicated to organizing for racial justice in education: the Education for Liberation Network and the Abolitionist Teaching Network.

CONTENTS

Foreword • ix

INTRODUCTION: #CurriculumSoWhite • 1

CHAPTER 1   Curricular Tools of Whiteness • 25

CHAPTER 2   The Iceberg: Racial Ideology and Curriculum • 63

CHAPTER 3   Reframing Understandings
of Race Within Teacher Education • 83

CHAPTER 4   Disrupting Whiteness in Teacher Education • 109

CHAPTER 5   Humanizing Racial Justice
in Teacher Education • 135

Acknowledgments • 171

Notes • 175

Index • 193

FOREWORD

The United States is not just racist; it is anti-Black. The word "racism" does not adequately describe the ways in which the US kills, destroys, and spirit murders Black people. As kihana miraya ross points out, racism "fails to fully capture what black people in this country are facing."[1] It has become a catch-all term used to explain the systemic denial of rights, jobs, housing, education, and healthcare to Black people. Yet the term "racism" does not include the extent of America's disdain, visceral hate, and disregard for Black life, Black love, Black empowerment, Black resistance, Black joy, and Black education.

The year 2020 will be recorded as a year of disdain for Black life. The ways in which anti-Blackness and racism showed up in the everyday lives of Black people and how we fought back are a testament to our cultural means of resistance, survival, abolition, and Black joy, which we take with us into formal and informal educational experiences. America's obsession with greed, violence, hate, and Black suffering always reaches into the most sacred spaces of American democracy, including schools. One of the most seductive features of White supremacy is the omitting and erasing of the history, culture, language, contributions, and humanity of all ethnicities and cultures that are not White, male, straight, and able-bodied. Beyond those identity markers, every other ethnicity has had to fight, protest, march, and petition to be included within public education. These struggles meant sending children of color into schools of anti-darkness, suffering, and structural erasure.

One way of erasing students of color, even while they gain access to schooling, was through the curriculum. For centuries, students of color have sat in classrooms never seeing their culture, history, or language. The life, love, and creativity of history has only been presented to students as the White man's visions, dreams, and contributions. To some, the fight to be included in school curriculum may seem over because ethnicities have been given superficial months to celebrate our prolific history within the confines of thirty days, or only twenty-eight for Black history. But we want, deserve, and demand more than a month at a time. Our histories and herstories are bigger, richer, and more complex than this country's compartmentalization of our lives into months and one-day celebrations of the culture and food that have nourished many of us, all while White supremacy and anti-Blackness attacked our souls.

What American schools fail to understand is that curriculum rich in the stories and lives of Black, Brown, and people of color humanizes not only students of color but White students as well. The work of decolonizing the curriculum helps decolonize all children's thinking, and that is what education for social justice should be. We cannot do the work of creating more socially just schools without removing curriculum that does not reflect people of color as human and the creators of our own lives and culture, who made contributions to this country and the world.

Too often teachers want to reflect a happy world to children, where no one was enslaved, no one was beaten, no families were separated, and White people never hurt anyone. These feel-good stories of White heroes and do-gooders uphold White supremacy and undermine the mental well-being of youth of color. To be frank, I am tired of seeing children, all children, opening up a textbook and reading about Black people as slaves and Native Americans as savages. I am even more appalled and angry when teachers do not see anything wrong with these representations.

What Bree Picower has done in this book is masterfully assemble the stories and the omnipresence of the #CurriclumSoWhite hashtag. *Reading, Writing, and Racism* tells the truth about America's racism and its disdain for people of color through the lens of curriculum. But this book is more than stories of Whiteness in education; it also provides a road map to justice, specifically to humanizing racial justice in teacher education. What Picower does, so beautifully and with such grace, is to outline how we strategize in communities to disrupt, agitate, and eliminate Whiteness within the curriculum and teacher education. This is no small task, and no book can address every issue, but *Reading, Writing, and Racism* comes close. Use this book as your guide, as your compass toward transforming not only teacher education but the lives of students of color to see themselves in powerful ways that restore, love, justice, and humanity.

BETTINA L. LOVE
ATLANTA, GEORGIA

#CURRICULUMSOWHITE

How easy, then, by emphasis and omission to make children
believe that every great soul the world ever saw was a white
man's soul; that every great thought the world ever knew was
a white man's thought; that every great deed the world ever
did was a white man's deed; that every great dream the world
ever sang was a white man's dream.[1]

—W. E. B. DU BOIS, 1920

There's #OscarsSoWhite and then there's
#CurriculumSoWhite. How curriculum in US public
schools remains centered on White middleclass norms.[2]

—DJANGO PARIS, @DJANGO _ PARIS, 2016

"How many slaves would be needed to equal at least 4 White people?"[3]

This was a homework question posed to middle school students in Kannapolis in 2019 following a lesson on the Three-Fifths Compromise. In 2018, an eighth-grade teacher at a Texas charter school asked her students to list "positive and negative aspects of slavery" as part of a unit called "The Lives of Slaves: A Balanced View."[4] Not to be outdone, a White public school teacher in the Bronx singled out her middle school Black students during a social studies lesson and had them lie on the classroom floor. She then put her foot on one child's back and announced, "See how it feels to be a slave?"[5]

These are just three examples of racist curriculum that have gone viral on social media. While these were the acts of individual educators, the problem is a systemic one, as widely used textbooks actively remove historical racism from the curriculum. For example, a McGraw-Hill textbook referred to enslaved Africans as "migrant workers,"[6] and Texas-approved textbooks removed Jim Crow, the Ku Klux Klan, and the role of slavery in the Civil War from its pages.[7] While some would see these examples as simply the result of "bad apple" teachers or outdated textbooks, in *Reading, Writing, and Racism*, I analyze such examples through a framework to understand how they are situated in historical racism and work to maintain current racial hierarchies. Popular culture may refer to reading, writing, and arithmetic as the "Three Rs" of education, but this book argues that racism is as inherent and basic to schooling as the Three Rs.

VIRAL RACIST CURRICULUM

Countless scholars, such as Carter G. Woodson, Gloria Ladson-Billings, James Loewen, Eve Tuck and Rúben Gaztambide-Fernández, Dolores Calderon, Prentice T. Chandler, Anthony Brown and Keffrelyn Brown, and LaGarrett King, have engaged thorough critiques of how racism and Eurocentrism have manifested themselves in a wide range of curricular resources.[8] This book follows that tradition, focusing specifically on examples of racist curriculum that have gone viral over social media in the last decade, represented by the hashtag #CurriculumSoWhite. This hashtag started in 2015 as a riff off of the #OscarsSoWhite hashtag, created by diversity and inclusion specialist April Reign, which called attention to the lack of nominees of Color at the Academy Awards. Taken up by race and education scholars such as Django Paris and organizations such as the NYC Coalition for Educational Justice, #CurriculumSoWhite calls attention to the ways in which Whiteness is present in schooling.

I have made the choice to focus on these viral examples because they are telling for many reasons. These singular examples reflect the toxicity of the entire body of school curricula. People outside of education rarely have a window into what happens behind classroom doors, so when these examples appear online for all to see, they call into question what other racial injustices are going on in schools. Additionally, the nature of the way the examples go viral follows a pattern that has implications for change. Typically, a parent or student recognizes that this one instance of schoolwork is problematic and posts it on Facebook or Twitter. For families, this homework assignment or textbook page might be one of the only tangible artifacts they have that illustrates how race is showing up in their children's education. These posts often focus only on the one particular lesson or the perpetrating teacher.

The analysis of #CurriculumSoWhite in this book situates these viral examples within their broader place in historical and structural racism. While the examples in the book focus on those that go viral, the analysis applies to all forms of racist curriculum. These racist curricular examples are not a new phenomenon attributable to changes in US political structure, as racism has always been implicated in curriculum and schooling. As expressed in the opening quote from W. E. B. Du Bois in 1920, "through emphasis and omission," children have long been educated through a Eurocentric lens. Rather than presenting the viral racist examples above as results of the poor judgment or implicit bias of individual teachers or curriculum developers, this book situates such examples of racist pedagogy, be they through emphasis, omission, or outright lies, in a broader context of historical and institutional racism and its role in US schooling.

What teachers choose to teach often represents their ways of thinking about race and how they have been socialized to understand difference through their families, the media, and the broader dominant culture. The book examines the relationship between individual teachers' racial beliefs and the curriculum they choose. These instructional decisions are influenced by and also reinforce racial hierarchies at a societal level. By lifting up teacher racial understandings and the impact they have on teachers' curricula, *Reading, Writing, and Racism* illuminates how racist beliefs are maintained over generations. Rather than using education as a vehicle to create a more equitable and just society, teachers whose understandings of race are unexamined instead, either purposefully or unconsciously, use their curriculum to indoctrinate the next generation with the same racist beliefs.

All teachers have the capacity to reproduce racism in their curriculum, so, interrogating understandings of race and racism are important acts for teachers of all races. Within my research on viral racist curriculum, however, it is clear that the majority of the perpetrators of these acts are White teachers. Therefore, the analysis of this book, and the strategies for change, focus on those using racist curriculum. While this is, arguably, centering Whiteness, it is a choice I made based on the statistics on White teachers in the field.[9] The teaching force of the United States is over 80 percent White, and almost half of US schools do not have a single teacher of Color on staff, even though students of Color now outnumber their White counterparts.[10] This is unlikely to shift dramatically, as it was shown that of ACT-tested graduates in 2014 who said they planned on pursuing an education major, 72 percent were White.[11] Adding to this dilemma is that new teachers are being prepared by teacher education faculty (including adjunct faculty) who are about 78 percent White.[12]

These statistics warrant teacher education to specifically address the ways in which White teachers and teacher educators carry their racial beliefs into the classroom. While it is necessary for teachers of all races to develop racial consciousness, the sheer numbers of White people in the field of teaching, coupled with their frequent lack of experience thinking about and addressing race, makes it essential to understand the ways in which White racial identity influences how they enact—and how they can reframe—their understandings of race. As a White professor who teaches and researches issues of race, I chose to focus this book on examining how White people enact racism so that we can learn how to dismantle it.

WHITE SOCIALIZATION

So how is it that White teachers who have graduated from accredited teacher education programs, been vetted by thoughtful search committees, and been hired to educate young people come into the classroom poised to perpetuate egregiously racist acts through their curriculum? In this section, I will provide an overview of some of the theoretical concepts that undergird this question. However, understanding how race and racism operate is complex and is the subject of many other books that I recommend reading in full for more detailed knowledge.[13] There is a deep and long tradition of scholars of Color, particularly Black scholars, who have written about race that informed my work, as cited throughout this book. If *Reading, Writing, and Racism* happens to be opening the door to your journey in understanding race, these endnotes serve as some of your next steps.

Teachers, like all members of society, are socialized into the mainstream ideology that governs a society. Cultural theorist Stuart Hall defines ideology as "the mental frameworks—the languages, the concepts, categories, imagery of thought, and the systems of representation—which different classes and social groups deploy in order to make sense of, figure out and render intelligible the way society works."[14] Hall contends that ideology "grips the minds of the masses" to become a political force that ultimately maintains power and domination. Ideology becomes the mainstream, commonsense ideas that shape how people see the world and explains how the values and beliefs of teachers find their way into the curriculum they develop or teach. Teachers teach what they believe about how the world works, and what they believe has been influenced by broader societal forces that serve to justify current social orders.

In the United States, the social order is based on racist hierarchies. This is also referred to as White supremacy, or a white supremacist society. As defined by scholar and journalist Robert Jensen:

> By "white supremacist," I mean a society whose founding is based in an ideology of the inherent superiority of white Europeans over non-whites, an ideology that was used to justify crimes against indigenous people and Africans that created the nation. That ideology also has justified legal and extralegal exploitation of every non-white immigrant group, and is used to this day to rationalize the racialized disparities in the distribution of wealth and well-being in this society. It is a society in which white people occupy most of the top positions in powerful institutions, with similar privileges available in limited ways to non-white people who fit themselves into white society.[15]

Within this system of White supremacy, *Whiteness* is the ideology and way of being in the world that is used to maintain it. *Whiteness* is not synonymous with *White people*; instead, it is the way in which people—generally White people—enact racism in ways that consciously and unconsciously maintain this broader system of White supremacy. While individual people of Color may also enact Whiteness, they do not benefit from the broader system of White supremacy in the ways that White people do. White supremacy is the *what*, White people are typically the *who*, and Whiteness is the *how*.

Whiteness relies on remaining masked in order to maintain the ideology of an equitable and democratic society. This concept is particularly important in the context of this book in which White teachers are not only unaware of a broader system of racism but also are unaware of their role in maintaining it. Whiteness theorists Joe L. Kincheloe and Shirley R. Steinberg contended that racial power dynamics are "so well hidden, so far removed from everyday consciousness, that even those who benefit from it are sometimes unaware if its existence." They argue that "such erasure often leads individuals from dominant race, class and gender groups into an uncritical complicity with socio-political structural power asymmetries and cultural manifestations of inequality."[16] White teachers, unaware of how their own beliefs have been socialized around race, become complicit in maintaining racism.

For some White people, the system remains masked because they do not realize that they have a racial identity, believing that people of Color are the only people with a race. This tendency to see White racial identity as the absence of race makes it difficult to have productive conversations because they become discussions about "others."[17] In my experience doing racial justice work in teacher education for over twenty years, I've found that most White people have never had a conversation with other White people about what it is like being White. Having lived primarily among other Whites, many Whites see their culture as just "normal," "American," or generally "bland." When asked to recognize themselves as White or part of a larger group, there is often a level of discomfort and defensiveness and a tendency to default to our ethnic, religious, or European identities instead.

For other White people, they believe that because they do not engage in explicitly racist acts that they are therefore outside of the system of racism. In the notes section, I recommend a number of resources that deconstruct this misconception of Whiteness and support White people in recognizing how we enact racism.[18] In *Me and White Supremacy*, Layla F. Saad categorized a variety of ways that White people behaviorly enact Whiteness, including but not limited to: silence, saviorism, exceptionalism, privilege, fragility, superiority, centering, apathy, stereotyping, tone policing, cultural appropriation, tokenism, and White feminism. *Dismantling Racism*, a workbook created by Kenneth Jones and Tema Okun, also includes a list of how Whiteness is manifested, such as perfectionism, sense of urgency, defensiveness, quantity over quality, worship of the written word, paternalism, either/or thinking, power hoarding, fear of open conflict, individualism, and objectivity.[19]

Because White people tend to categorize only explicit hate crimes or racial slurs as racist, we often do not recognize how all of these other manifestations either consciously or unconsciously find their way into how we engage in the world. It is often because of these ways Whiteness is masked that seemingly caring White teachers perpetuate racism in their curriculum. In describing typical preservice teachers, author Sherry Marx points out that while White teachers may appear to be different from the stereotype of hood-wearing White supremacists, their "brand of racism" is just as dangerous.

> In fact they were much the opposite; they were lovely young women devoted to spending their careers tolerantly and benevolently working with "all children." However, one could argue that the ways in which they perpetuated racism were even more destructive than the hateful, violent rants of a White supremacist.

After all, White teachers number in the millions in this country and the brand of racism they/we perpetuate is viewed as helpful, knowledgeable, and in the best interests of children.[20]

Such "lovely" White teachers have been socialized to believe in a world absent of the myriad manifestations of Whiteness, as structures of White supremacy have been hidden from them through their own education. Teachers were at one point students on the receiving end of curriculum that, as analyzed by many critical race scholars, has been found to be Eurocentric, providing flawed and innacurate information about people of Color, particularly Black people.[21] Because of their own socialization and education, curriculum that perpetuates historic falsehoods align with teachers' incomplete understandings of race. It follows that they would unquestioningly pass this along to their own students through the kind of viral racist curriculum examined in this book.

Current racist curriculum should therefore be examined not by the educators' individual intention but by the way it functions to maintain the permanence of racism both in and out of school.[22] In his book *Stamped from the Beginning*, Ibram X. Kendi explains that we often think that racism is a result of ignorance. He posits, however, that White historical self-interest leads to racist policies, which then leads to the construction of racist ideas to justify the policies, which then results in ignorance and hate, keeping the cycle in place.[23] Using this flow of power, teachers who teach racist curriculum are not simply acting out of implicit bias or racial ignorance as is often assumed. Rather, they are complicit in keeping a broader racist system in place. They do this through the construction of a racist curriculum that functions to justify racism by reproducing and instilling racist ideas in the next generation, keeping White supremacy in place.

As will be seen in chapter 1, the viral artifacts of #Curriculum-SoWhite that turned up in my research were almost exclusively racist toward Black and Indigenous people. Therefore, I will often use the term *Black, Indigenous, and people of Color*, commonly abbreviated as BIPOC, throughout this book. *BIPOC* is a term that has emerged to highlight that while racism impacts all people of Color, it is critical to distinguish the ways in which it often most violently and aggressively targets Black and Indigenous people.[24]

The overabundance of racist curriculum toward these two groups in particular reveals the legacy of settler colonialism and anti-Blackness in the United States. As scholars Anne Bonds and Joshua Inwood explain, "A settler colonial perspective illuminates the interconnections between colonization and anti-black and anti-indigenous racisms and understands them as an ongoing structure rather than a series of historic events."[25] While the origins of Indigenous displacement and chattel slavery are historical, the ripples of this history do not disappear. Instead, traces of these arrangements are made evident through #CurriculumSoWhite. Again, these examples of racist curriculum must be seen as broader than the individual racism of one teacher. Instead, they represent the larger project of maintaining the social conditions of settler colonialism, Whiteness, and White supremacy by reproducing these historical legacies and cementing anti-Black and anti-Indigenous racial ideologies in the imaginations of new generations of learners.

FOUR I'S OF OPPRESSION

What makes #CurriculumSoWhite particularly insidious in maintaining racism is that when used by educators, the curriculum operates at the intersection of four levels of oppression. A popular framework that grassroots and social justice organizations use these days for teaching about inequality is called the Four I's of Oppression. This framework asserts that all forms of oppression operate on four overlapping levels: *ideological, institutional, interpersonal/individual,* and *internalized*. My colleague Tanya Maloney and I use the Four I's as the organizing framework of the program we co-direct, the Newark Teacher Project. NTP is an example of a teacher education program that centers racial justice through a humanizing framework. (More characteristics about racial justice teacher education programs will be shared in chapters 4 and 5.)

After we presented the framework during a racial literacy professional development workshop, a Black participant commented that it should not only be framed around oppression, but also around how superiority operates at all four levels so as to focus on the perpetrators of oppression and not just on the targets. As such, we started referring to it as the Four I's of Oppression and Advantage. For all the ways that the Four I's negatively impact those marginalized by oppression, there is an equal and opposite privilege assigned to those advantaged by that identity marker. To understand how inequality operates and can be dismantled, we must focus on the mechanisms and impact of both oppression and advantage.

Oftentimes, we can parse out a single level on which oppression/advantage happens. For example, believing that White people are inherently smarter or more deserving is ideological racial advantage; disproportionate access to quality education based on race is institutional racial advantage; telling a racist joke is interpersonal/individual racial oppression; and holding feelings that Eurocentric beauty standards such as paler skin and straight hair are more desirable is internalized racial oppression and advantage.[26]

However, unlike these single-level examples, #CurriculumSoWhite operates across all four levels. I'll play this out with a story of a former student, Dawn, who I will share more about in chapter 2. Dawn grew up in an Italian American community and was socialized to believe that her family was successful because they worked hard. To Dawn, people of Color who weren't as successful or who hadn't achieved the American Dream were simply lazy. The ideology of the American Dream shaped how Dawn thought about racism.

This *ideological* understanding formed the way she thought about racism—believing it was a thing of the past and that people of Color, particularly Black people, were complaining about something that no longer existed. As a teacher and as a White person carrying this racist ideology, Dawn had access to *institutional* power—for example, she had the capacity to refer students of Color to special education or White students to gifted and talented programs. She also had *institutional* power over what she chose to teach, and she chose to teach an inaccurate version of history using #CurriculumSoWhite. Her *ideological* beliefs shaped her curricular choices, as we will see in chapter 2. While she worked as an individual to develop what she would teach, her curriculum upheld *institutional* and *ideological* oppression by telling an inaccurate history of how racism has been "solved." At the *internalized* level, this curriculum inculcates her students into also believing that racism is over. Her White students could therefore *internalize* that anti-racism is unnecessary, and her students of Color might *internalize* that they and their families are responsible for any oppression they may experience. Through her *institutional* power over curriculum, Dawn as an *individual* passed on her *ideology* that her students then *internalized*. When employed by teachers, #CurriculumSoWhite is especially nefarious because rather than operating at just the teacher's individual level, it maintains Whiteness on all four levels.

TEACHER EDUCATION AS A SPACE TO TRANSFORM RACIAL IDEOLOGY

Given the enormity of the scope of Whiteness, where then are the moments of intervention to transform teachers' understandings of race in the hopes that they do not maintain systems of racism through the transmission of racist ideas? Whose role and responsibility is it to interrupt #CurriculumSoWhite? I argue that teachers create curriculum that flows from their ideology—in other words, educators teach what they believe. It would follow then that sites for disruption are the spaces in which they learn to teach, as these can also become the places in which they rethink their beliefs.

Teacher education provides a place in which aspiring educators learn the art and science of teaching. As an institution, it has the potential to disrupt #CurriculumSoWhite by taking seriously the relationship between what teachers think and what they teach. Some programs do make an attempt to train teachers in multicultural or culturally relevant curriculum, but this is often done in a way that assumes that all aspiring teachers might be open to such approaches.[27] In truth, preservice teachers must excavate what education scholar Yolanda Sealey-Ruiz refers to as the "archeology of the self."[28] Without in-depth self-examination and reflection on how issues of race, class, and identity play out in preservice teachers' understandings of others, efforts to prepare anti-racist teachers can end up as the equivalent to slapping a coat of paint on the wall when the foundation is rotten. Unless teachers' underlying ideology is disrupted from dominant racial paradigms, this coat of paint and the resulting curriculum ends up being superficial at best (for example, George Washington Carver discovered peanuts! Rosa Parks sat down!) and outrageously racist at worst.[29]

Take this example, which will be revisited in chapter 1: A 2016 eighth-grade mathematics test given at Burns Middle School in

Mobile, Alabama. Assigned by the math teacher, one question on the test read: "Tyrone knocked up 4 girls in the gang. There are 20 girls in his gang. What is the exact percentage of the girls Tyrone knocked up?" Another question informed students that "Dwayne pimps 3 ho's" and asked students to figure out "how many tricks each of the hookers must turn in a day to support Dwayne's crack habit."[30] Some might erroneously interpret that the teacher thought she was using a culturally relevant perspective, yet these questions reveal that her core beliefs about her students are steeped in racist stereotypes. Until teacher education is ready to dig deeper to address the beliefs of teachers like this one, attempts at curricular reforms will not interrupt racist curriculum.

TENSIONS AND INTENTIONS AS A WHITE SCHOLAR WRITING ABOUT RACE

Having grown up as a White person with racial and economic privilege, I was not immune from being socialized to have mainstream understandings of race as a young person.[31] However, I was fortunate to have had a variety of professional experiences and relationships that helped me start the lifelong process of examining and reframing my understandings about race. My journey is one of a trajectory of working in educational settings run for and by Black people. From working in afterschool programs in New York City, Michigan, and San Francisco; to teaching at Prescott Elementary, a predominately Black school in Oakland, California, that was the center of the "Ebonics debate" in the late 1990s; to eventually studying Whiteness in education as a scholar, I have been in settings in which Black people have generously taken the time to invest in my development within educational settings that center racial justice.[32]

Through these experiences, I was given the opportunity to learn valuable lessons that helped reshape the way I saw the world, the first of which was that White people don't have the answers. To address racial justice, it is necessary to listen and learn from people oppressed by racial injustice. Having volunteered in high school in centers that were "serving" Black children but were run by White adults, I soon gained an appreciation of the importance of Black leadership. In all of these settings, race was explicitly on the table. Having opportunities to develop meaningful and reciprocal relationships with my Black coworkers turned friends, hearing and learning from their perspectives on issues of race, developing the ability to participate in racially charged discussions, and working in environments run by and for Black people all played a significant role in shaping my racial analysis. I am grateful to be able to continue to be part of a multiracial community of critically conscious scholars, in which we lovingly support and develop our vision and actions for educational racial justice. I share this brief summary of my journey, not to paint a portrait of myself as a "White exception" but to show that particular experiences have the potential to disrupt certain ideologies of Whiteness.

My last year teaching at Prescott Elementary, my mentor teacher, Carrie Secret, pulled me aside and told me that although she loved me, she didn't need me to be there. She let me know that it was my responsibility to take what I had learned at Prescott and to go work with White people—basically, to go get my cousins. As a classroom teacher, and as a person, I had learned that when Ms. Secret talks, you listen. Now, having been a teacher educator for almost twenty years, my work centers upon supporting teachers, particularly White teachers, to have similar opportunities to reframe their understandings about race prior to going into the classroom.

As a White person doing this work, there is never a point of "arrival," and I continue to reflect on my racial identity, navigating certain tensions and setting intentions. Part of the process of moving toward anti-racism is constant self-examination and a questioning of what work I should or should not be doing given my positionality as someone who ultimately benefits from the system of racism. I also notice this questioning of self as a pattern with the White teachers I work with as they begin the journey of becoming more racially conscious (e.g., "How can I teach about race as a White person with all Black students?"). I've come to believe that this self-consciousness is a part of the process of trying to be a responsible White person in racial justice work. Part of the culture of Whiteness is to believe that we have all the answers and that we have the right to do anything our hearts desire. Therefore, part of grappling with my own Whiteness is to destabilize this tendency by monitoring my reactions, my interactions, who I gravitate toward and why, how I engage with others, when to speak up, when to lean back, when to say yes, and when to say no, and so on.

In trying to navigate my own White identity in the field, I engage in this self-examination while also trying to be accountable to people of Color about what my role in this work should be. Because people of Color are not a monolith, there are a variety of ideas from different circles engaged in racial justice about the role of White people in anti-racist work. I have taken direction from Alicia Garza, one of the three Black women who founded the Black Lives Matter (BLM) movement, who explains that Black Lives Matter asks non-Black people to "not just stand in solidarity with [#BLM], but to investigate the ways in which anti-Black racism is perpetuated in [our] own communities."[33] My teaching and writing responds to this demand to uncover racism within my community of teacher education and to think about how it can instead be a lever of change.

Some race scholars of Color make it clear that because racism benefits and is perpetuated by Whites that White people need to step up and take on the work of ending it. This is part of the responsibility White people carry. Speaking to this issue, the founders of Black Lives Matter write, "We remain persistent in urging non-Black, anti-racist communities to organize themselves and their people in the fight for Black lives and liberation. The turbulent road to civil rights has long been paved with the support and resistance of allies and their significance in this struggle cannot be overstated."[34] Scholar Bettina Love calls attention to the difference between allies and "co-conspirators," calling for White people to go beyond performative allyship of just appearing "woke," to instead take risks that put themselves on the line for BIPOC and for racial justice.[35]

For me personally, the term *ally* has always fallen short because it assumes the struggle for racial justice is a horizontal one in which White people should do something about racism on behalf of people of Color. This is a slippery slope into saviorism, which reinforces a dangerous narrative of viewing myself as a "good" White person for engaging in "charitable" activities that might benefit individual people of Color without questioning how power is operating. Allyship relegates racial justice to the interpersonal level of the Four I's, which is insufficient because it does not engage in dismantling institutional racism. Moving from *ally* to *co-conspirator* shifts the target of anti-racist action from individual people of Color to the unjust system, driving White people from charity to solidarity.

At the same time that people of Color are calling for White people to be co-conspirators, there is also rightful frustration that White anti-racist activists receive recognition and career advancement from talking about race more than people of Color do. White people who do racial justice work, such as Tim Wise and Robin DiAngelo, are often taken to task for the opportunities and careers they have gained talking about racism. Black sex educator and writer Ericka Hart posted on Twitter: "White people should NOT be capitalizing off of racial justice, as they are the very reason racial justice is needed. Any money white folks make from racial justice should be going to Black people ONLY. I'm looking at you Chelsea Handler,

Tim Wise and DiAngelo."[36] This post garnered over 13,000 likes in a few days and prompted Sonya Renee Taylor, executive director and author of *The Body Is Not an Apology*, to upload a compelling video analysis to Instagram.[37] She made an analogy to the fact that pharmaceutical companies not only created and profit from the opioid crisis but also created and profit from the drug that can stop an opioid overdose. Taylor pointed out that White people similarly created and profit from racism and therefore should not be profiting from dismantling it.

I am working to navigate the tensions in these messages. As writer Tre Johnson wrote in a brilliant op-ed for the *Washington Post*, entitled "When Black People Are in Pain, White People Just Join Bookclubs": "The confusing, perhaps contradictory advice on what white people should do probably feels maddening. To be told to step up, no step back, read, no listen, protest, don't protest, check on black friends, leave us alone, ask for help or do the work—it probably feels contradictory at times. And yet, you'll figure it out."[38] Figuring it out, as Johnson suggests, is part of the work of being a White person involved in racial justice and is nothing compared to what it means to navigate racism for BIPOC. As Johnson continues, "Black people have been similarly exhausted making the case for jobs, freedom, happiness, justice, equality and the like. It's made us dizzy, but we've managed to find the means to walk straight."

Over time, I have developed certain principles that I try to stand by to balance these different perspectives. Like lines in the sand, they occasionally get crossed, erased, and redrawn as new thinking emerges. These principles are specifically about my work on racism, as I also research other topics within the field of education such as broader issues of social justice, teacher activism, and elementary education.

Here are two of my principles that currently guide my action as a

White person engaged in racial justice work. Because of the history of White anthropologists "studying" BIPOC and essentializing their culture, my first principle is that I instead keep my gaze on Whiteness. For example, rather than position children of Color as research subjects, I ask questions about the impact that the overrepresentation of White teachers has on students of Color. My concern is with the ways that White people harm students of Color, rather than to contribute to the piles of problematic research that perpetuates a deficit view of children of Color.

My second principle is that when asked to present or consult about racism, I aim to co-present with a colleague who is BIPOC whenever possible. If I present or consult alone, it is at the request of people of Color, and only after suggesting that I work with a co-facilitator. This isn't a performative move for optics; the work is more powerful when done collectively. We bring different perspectives to the table and provide participants with more opportunities to relate to us so they can hear the different ways that racism operates. When writing about racism and how it impacts BIPOC, I aim to coauthor with people of Color. My single-authored works, like this book, are about Whiteness specifically or about other aspects of teaching such as social justice education or teacher activism.

With regard to compensation for racial justice consulting opportunities that I am presented with, I am working to come up with principles that feel right in light of some of the debates on White people's roles within racial justice. Part of what provides me with the opportunity for these paid opportunities is the work that I have been doing in the field for twenty years. However, another part of what has enabled me to be where I am is race and class privilege. For example, I had the privilege of being able to take volunteer positions in high school working with children that provided me with the experience needed to get education-based jobs in college. Out of college, I was promoted over two coworkers of Color to direct an after-school program, despite the fact that I didn't have the early childhood credits required of the position at the time. I didn't realize then that this was because of racism, but now that I know it, how do I take responsibility for the boosts these privileges gave my career to get me where I am now? While the country debates national reparations, I wonder, what do personal reparations look like?

One strategy is to donate portions of fees from paid racial justice work to organizations engaged in racial justice led by BIPOC. Robin DiAngelo, author of *White Fragility* and a White anti-racist scholar, explains this method of accountability: "A percentage of my income goes to racial justice organizations led by people of color. Two-thirds of net income raised from my public workshops go directly to local racial justice organizations led by people of color, so I am not making more than those local organizations I am donating to."[39]

As part of grappling with this, I recognize that my institution, Montclair State University, supported me with a sabbatical that provided me with time and compensation to write this book. Following the lead of Carla Shalaby, author of the brilliant book *Troublemakers*, I have donated my advance (outside of overhead) and will donate 100 percent of royalties of this book to two grassroots, racial justice education organizations led by people of Color. The Education for Liberation Network, an organization I have been involved with for over a decade, is "a national coalition of teachers, community activists, researchers, youth, and parents who believe a good education should teach people—particularly low-income youth and youth of Color—how to understand and challenge the injustices their communities face." The Abolitionist Teaching Network, started by Bettina Love, aims to "develop and support educators to fight injustice within their schools and communities."[40]

While donations to these organizations may responsibly address my racial accountability, it lifts up questions in light of class privilege. As a full-time professor with benefits, I have the means to position my writing and consulting as supplemental to my salary. This arrangement problematically sets up a dynamic in which only White people with economic privilege can be seen as engaging "responsibly" in racial justice work. Under a racial capitalist system, there are no clean solutions. Just as there are multiple perspectives on White people's roles in anti-racism work, I recognize that there will be a variety of reactions about these principles of engagement, but my aim is to make my intentions and tensions visible and to be as accountable as possible.

DESCRIPTION OF CHAPTERS

The introduction and chapter 1 of this book open with an examination of how curriculum functions to maintain dominant power structures through a reinvestment in Whiteness. Education has the potential to function as both a tool that reproduces inequality or a space of liberation and resistance. To be a space of freedom, teachers must create room for students to engage with the accurate historical record of colonization, enslavement, oppression, and inequality that has shaped the present context of our society. This allows students to grapple with hard truths and learn the complexity of oppression in order to dismantle it. In chapter 1, I examine how education functions instead to maintain racial hierarchies by hiding the realities of oppression through the telling of a falsified story of American progress. I do this by applying a framework I previously developed called Tools of Whiteness specifically to curriculum to demonstrate how teaching and content choices can serve to maintain White supremacy.

After understanding how this curriculum maintains racism, chapter 2 looks at how teachers' racial ideology is linked to what they teach by using data collected from almost two decades of preparing and supporting educators to teach from a racial justice stance. In this chapter, I share four case studies of novice White teachers to demonstrate how their personal experiences and understandings about race find their way into their curriculum. I show the pathway from these teachers' ideological roots to the curriculum they ultimately taught, mitigated by how they responded to anti-racist teacher education. By highlighting teachers' reflections about race and analyzing the curricular projects they create, findings indicate that there is a powerful relationship between teachers' ideological understandings and their capacity to reproduce or resist #CurriculumSoWhite.

Given the findings, chapter 3 argues that addressing teachers' racial ideology provides hope in interrupting the proliferation of racist curricula seen in chapter 1. This chapter explores the very specific ways that White teachers must reframe their understandings about race in order to advance racial justice rather than reproduce racism. This chapter dives into preservice teachers' reflections about their journeys toward anti-racist teaching and how they had to rethink their lifetime of socialization around institutional, interpersonal, ideological, and internalized racism.

In order for teacher education to support the kinds of racial reframing examined in chapter 3, schools of education need to restructure themselves to advance racial justice. To facilitate the kind of transformation to teachers' racial ideology needed to interrupt curricular Tools of Whiteness, teacher education needs to make a commitment to advance racial justice. While this sounds great in theory, what does it actually look like in practice? To answer this question, chapters 4 and 5 delve into the structures and principles that guide five teacher education programs at institutes of higher education that all center racial justice. These chapters provide a window into possible program designs, highlighting how a focus on racial justice can be built into programs across the teacher education pipeline—from admission to induction.

The late educational policy professor Jean Anyon conceptualized "Radical Possibilities" as a way of addressing overwhelming socioeconomic inequality through social movements, recognizing that social change has historically been achieved only through collective struggle.[41] Africana history professor Robin D. G. Kelley wrote about the concept of "Freedom Dreams" as a way to envision a new world coming out of the Black Radical Tradition involving "collective action, personal self-transformation and will."[42] Both concepts have been taken up by activists and movements in keeping an eye not just on the issues that need to be fought against but also the new configurations of what we are in the struggle for. Radical Possibilities and Freedom Dreams are key to this book's larger project of moving away from schools as spaces that maintain systems of racism and instead offers us an opportunity to imagine together how education can be a place for liberatory change. By examining the who, what, why, and how of racial justice teacher education, this book provides radical possibilities for transforming schools into spaces for freedom dreaming.

CHAPTER 1

CURRICULAR TOOLS OF WHITENESS

Honey, if you want to clean the house, you have to see the dirt.

—LOUISE HAY

CURRICULAR TOOLS OF WHITENESS

In this chapter, I share examples of curriculum used in K–12 schools that publicly came to light because of the outrage and organizing of parents of Color who came across their children's assignments and took to social media to share their righteous indignation. As a trigger warning, the examples of curriculum in this chapter are distressing. They range from potentially easy-to-miss examples to violent and traumatic assignments. The majority of the examples in my research are anti-Black in nature and deal with the teaching of enslavement in particular. My goal in sharing these examples is not to re-traumatize BIPOC or to make White people feel bad, but rather to bring to light the breadth and depth of how racism is perpetuated through everyday, real assignments in K–12 schools. This way we can name, disrupt, and change it. As motivational author Louise Hay once said, "Honey, if you want to clean the house, you have to see the dirt." This chapter is the dirt.

I have been collecting social media posts of racist curricula for years and have organized these examples into a framework for understanding how these are more than random, singular examples of poor judgment by individual "bad apple" teachers. They also aren't a reflection of the turn toward explicit racism under the forty-fifth US president. Rather, these examples function as what I have named Tools of Whiteness because they use a variety of strategies to socialize students to internalize existing racist ideologies, ensuring that racial hierarchies are maintained through the education system.

In previous work, I lay out a framework of Tools of Whiteness, which reveals scripted responses used to maintain teachers' investment in White supremacy.[1] White supremacy requires certain ideologies to remain in place in order to maintain power. Just as tools allow a job to be done more effectively or efficiently, Tools of Whiteness facilitate the job of maintaining and supporting the thoughts, language, and ways of acting that uphold structures of White supremacy. In other words, Tools of Whiteness function to deny, evade, subvert, or avoid ways of analyzing racism as a form of oppression.

Given that 82 percent of US teachers are White, the very people who have benefitted from racism and have themselves been educated to hold racist ideas are the ones tasked with moving the next generation toward reproduction or resistance of racism.[2] Rather than move toward racial justice, some teachers both consciously and unconsciously use curricular Tools of Whiteness to revise the historical record in ways that preserve the idea of Whiteness as good, superior, and ever present. When educators teach in this way, curriculum and instruction become projects in which ideologies of racism are reproduced in the minds of the next generation. While the individual educator using curricular Tools of Whiteness may not intend or be conscious of this role they are playing, the consequences remain the same. The following chart lays out the curricular Tools of Whiteness; the sections that follow provide classroom examples that demonstrate how each tool operates.

CURRICULAR TOOLS OF WHITENESS

- White Out
- No One Is to Blame
- Not That Bad

- All Things Being Equal
- White Gaze

- Embedded Stereotypes
- Racist Reproduction

CURRICULAR TOOL OF WHITENESS: WHITE OUT

In order to maintain racial hierarchies with Whiteness at the top, curricula using this tool cement Whiteness as normal, innocent, and ever present. In order for schools to be places of liberation, teachers would have to tell the full picture about the history of whose land the US was founded on and with whose labor. This would require teachers to portray White people as the perpetrators of violence against BIPOC.

Most curricular tools of Whiteness function to avoid teaching the history of the formation of the United States accurately. The White Out tool specifically achieves this by simply not including people of Color *at all*. When teachers choose this tool, they reinforce Whiteness in three different ways. First, by erasing the history of oppression that BIPOC have faced at the hands of White people, teachers affirm the post-racial idea that all people are on an even playing field. Second, by erasing the sheer existence of BIPOC from the learning experiences of all students, teachers send messages to children about who is deemed valuable or expendable, reinforcing racial hierarchies. Finally, by removing the accomplishments and resistance movements of BIPOC, especially in light of the oppression they faced, teachers block avenues for self-love or pride for students of Color.

Bill Bigelow, teacher and editor of the social justice education journal *Rethinking Schools*, published an article about his experience with the curricular White Out tool and how he reframed it.[3] He told his fifth-grade students about how some presidents had been en-slavers, which sparked their curiosity about which presidents specifi-cally. They began to research their question by looking through their dictionaries, social studies textbooks, kid-friendly websites, encyclo-pedias, and other sources—which, in keeping with the White Out tool, made no mention, or provided little or unclear information, of this aspect of presidential history. This omission of factual infor-mation demonstrates how this tool maintains the dominant narra-tive of the founding fathers as universally good. It also perpetuates the myth that the United States was founded in ways that represent freedom and equality for "all," despite the very real ways that racial oppression was key to this story.

Rather than allow this White Out tool to go unacknowledged, Bigelow encouraged his students to become "textbook detectives," which taught them how to identify and critically analyze historical White Outs. As a culmination, he had the students write letters to the textbook companies sharing their research data and demanding that they rewrite their books. When asked why the textbook com-panies omit this information, Bigelow's students responded: "They're stupid"; "They don't want us kids to know the truth"; "They think we're too young to know"; and "They don't know themselves." While Bigelow was able to support his students to see through and under-stand why publishers might white this information out, many teach-ers haven't been trained to be "textbook detectives" themselves, leaving this tool in play.

As seen in this example, it is often the omissions in textbooks and children's educational materials that are most heavily impli-cated in the White Out tool. In 2019, a New York City parent activ-ist group, the NYC Coalition for Educational Justice, issued a report called *Diverse City, White Curriculum: The Exclusion of People of Color from English Language Arts in NYC Schools*.[4] Partnered with researchers from New York University's Metropolitan Center for Research on Equity and the Transformation of Schools, the report examined 1,200 books across fifteen commonly used curricula and booklists, from 3-K and pre-K through eighth grade.[5] By looking at the racial background of both title characters as well as curricular authors, they found that while only 15 percent of New York City public school students are White, the characters in the most commonly used books are 52 percent White and the book authors are 84 percent White. In fact, they found that elementary books featured more animal characters than Black, Asian, or Latinx characters combined.[6] Megan Hester, director of the Education Justice Research and Organizing Collaborative, explained in responding to the report: "Children's books have traditionally played a role in socialization—teaching children how to think, how to act, and how to feel about themselves, others, and the world. Unfortunately, the erasure, dehumanization, marginalization, and whitewashing of people of Color have been a persistent part of that tradition."[7] When children are exposed to the White Out tool, they are being taught more than early literacy; they also are being presented with messages of both superiority and inferiority.

Children's and young adult literature play an important role in the development of young people's understanding of the world. Children's literature expert Rudine Sims Bishop developed the popular metaphor of windows and mirrors to describe representation in literature.[8] Ideally, there should be a mix of books that can serve both as opportunities for children of all racial identities to see their experiences mirrored back to them and as windows to see the world beyond themselves. Without this mix, what does it mean, then, for White children to be hyper-visible to themselves and others and for children of Color to learn in a mirror-less world in which they do not exist? Bishop explains, "When children cannot find themselves reflected in the books they read, or when the images they see are distorted, negative, or laughable, they learn a powerful lesson about how they are devalued in the society of which they are a part."[9] The White Out tool teaches this lesson through the omission of BIPOC from curricular materials.

CURRICULAR TOOL OF WHITENESS: NO ONE IS TO BLAME

While the White Out tool omitted people of Color, the following tools do portray BIPOC, but in distorted and problematic ways. Similar to the White Out tool, teachers use the No One Is to Blame tool to avoid assigning responsibility to White people for historical atrocities. In this case, teachers build curricula that include BIPOC, but the stories are told with no victims and no perpetrators. This maintains the dominant ideology of White people as benevolent, good, and innocent and paints a picture of an even playing field. This omission of blame encourages students to see atrocious acts as naturally occurring—as just "human nature" in which oppression occurs randomly and without pattern. Teachers use this tool to reframe and justify historical acts by providing explanations that do not involve power, resulting in a false and sanitized version of history that protects the reputation of White people.

Figure 1 is adapted from a textbook that uses the No One Is to Blame tool.[11] It is a snapshot taken by Coby Burren, a freshman in a Texas high school, from a McGraw-Hill textbook used in his geography class.[12] Under a map labeled "Patterns of Immigration," the caption reads "The Atlantic Slave Trade between the 1500s and 1800s brought millions of workers from Africa to the southern United States to work on agricultural plantations." Coby sent the photo to his mother, Roni Dean-Burren, who posted it on Facebook, where it went viral. In her Facebook post, Dean-Burren draws attention to

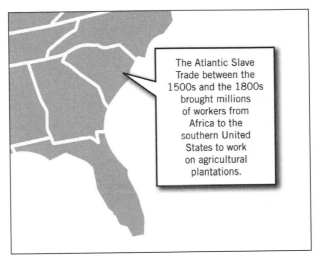

Figure 1. *Textbook example of Atlantic slave trade with no slave traders. Source:* Teks World Geography Student Edition (McGraw-Hill, 2015).[10]

how Africans transported to America against their will are framed as "immigrant workers" rather than as enslaved people. She points out that the textbook indicates that English and European people came as indentured servants to work for little or no pay but makes no similar mention for enslaved Africans, referring to them instead as "workers" or "immigrants."[13]

The publishers erase the violence of enslavement and how slave traders hunted and stole family members before exporting them from Africa to America, where they were sold as property to Europeans. By using the No One Is to Blame tool, the textbook authors not only misrepresent the forced migration of enslaved Africans as voluntary, but also they frame it so passively as to remove any oppressors. Who brought these "workers" to the agricultural plantations? How? Why? None of that is mentioned in this framing. This glaring omission of the role of Europeans in the trans-Atlantic slave trade reinforces the framing of White people as innocent and good in the American story of progress. This curricular Tool of Whiteness glosses over this historical atrocity, leaving not only no victims, but also no perpetrators.

In a similar use of the No One Is to Blame tool, a Canadian textbook has a section called "Moving Out" that stated: "When the European settlers arrived, they needed land to live on.[14] The First Nations people agreed to move to different areas to make room for the new settlements."[15] The book continues: "The First Nations people moved to reserves, where they could live undisturbed by the hustle and bustle of the settlers." This textbook uses the No One Is to Blame tool to frame colonization as an "agreement" between settlers and Indigenous people, masking the reality of settler colonialism, "which is the specific formation of colonialism in which the colonizer comes to stay, making himself the sovereign, and the arbiter of citizenship, civility, and knowing."[16] Instead of naming and grappling with settler colonialism, the textbook authors fictionalize a mutually beneficial arrangement in which settlers received land and First Nations people conceivably continued their way of life peacefully and undisturbed.

As demonstrated throughout this chapter, all of the examples of curricular Tools of Whiteness that I came across in my research, including the two examples above, distort the shared history and experiences of African Americans, Native Americans, and European people. This is not a coincidence, as Indigenous studies and education scholars Eve Tuck and Rubén A. Gaztambide-Fernández explain:

> In North America, settler colonialism operates through a triad of relationships, between the (white [but not always]) settlers, the Indigenous inhabitants, and chattel slaves who are removed from their homelands to work stolen land. . . . For settlers to live on

and profit from land, they must eliminate Indigenous peoples, and extinguish their historical, epistemological, philosophical, moral and political claims to land. Land, in being settled, becomes property. Settlers must also import chattel slaves, who must be kept landless, and who also become property, to be used, abused, and managed.[17]

These two textbook examples are implicated in this broader settler colonial project, maintaining White innocence in the story of how land and labor were acquired through "agreements" and "immigration" rather than genocide and enslavement. With no oppressor depicted, students internalize the dominant ideology of the natural order of our highly stratified society. One of my former students, Linda, demonstrated this idea of a natural order of domination when, in claiming why we should not teach about racism in schools, she said, "I think that there is always a group that is going to dominate another group of people. You know, whether it's Whites over African Americans or Indians over whoever." Linda framed domination as an aspect of human nature and was able to disconnect Whites from the oppressor position by offering other possibilities of dominant groups (although she could not actually name any other than "whoever").

Linda's way of thinking about oppression was likely made possible by her former teachers and their curriculum that also used the No One Is to Blame tool to obscure historical arrangements. As an educator, Linda is now able to continue this broader historical project of maintaining White innocence through curricula like the ones above. Adding insult to injury is the fact that these examples of curricular Tools of Whiteness are literally *textbook* examples. They passed through multiple editors, writers, review boards, editorial boards, and so on before being printing and distributed.

Individual teachers such as Linda do not have to create or question anything; they are handed the curricular Tools of Whiteness that align with their own ideology that they then seamlessly pass on to their students.

Similar to the way that teacher Bill Bigelow taught his students to recognize and analyze instances of White Out, teacher Laura Whooley posted on Facebook to share a similar example of how to educate children to speak back regarding the No One Is to Blame tool.[18] Her students were using a McGraw-Hill companion textbook when they came across the following sentence: "As more farmers grew tobacco, they needed more enslaved Africans to do the work." Rather than read this sentence and move on, Ms. Whooley and her students homed in on the word "needed." She used this teachable moment to support her students in understanding the dynamics of greed, money, and power in the arrangement of chattel slavery, how framing matters, and how to take action. She had her students write letters to McGraw-Hill sharing their analysis and concerns.

Fourth-grader Caroline wrote, "When it says 'needed' I think that is not really correct. When the wealthy people bought enslaved Africans, they didn't really *need* it. They *wanted* it. You see, the white people could've done all the work themselves, but they *wanted* slaves to do it." Caroline continued with her recommendation to the publisher: "You should replace needed with wanted. It's more realistic. And because when the 3rd graders come to 4th grade and see THAT, they are gonna think it's totally fine to enslave people because they NEED it." Caroline not only understood the power dynamic at play, she also named the role that the textbook plays in indoctrinating children to believe racial oppression.

Another student, Laurel, compellingly added, "1. No one needs slaves in this world. 2. Plantation owners could have done the work themselves instead of sitting on their lazy butts. 3. If they *need*

slaves, I *need* a pet panda." By calling to attention one simple verb—
needed—in a companion textbook, Ms. Whooley interrupted the
transmission of the idea that the enslavement of Africans was a logi-
cal and necessary solution to European economic desires. By teaching her students that in fact, someone was to blame, she provided a
significant example of the power teachers have to transform, rather
than reproduce, racist ideology.

CURRICULAR TOOL OF WHITENESS: NOT THAT BAD

When teachers use the Not That Bad tool, they aim to downplay
the horrific nature of past oppressions by promoting a sanitized picture of history, thereby maintaining White innocence. By convincing students that events like slavery or colonization were Not That
Bad, teachers propagate a false narrative of what it means to live
under oppressive circumstances, masking children's ability to understand current inequality. Minimizing the reality of how White
people inflicted racial violence on Black people under the institution
of slavery enables White people to claim that Black people and other
people of Color are playing the race card by obscuring the reality of
how racism operates to maintain the suffering of BIPOC.

In 2015, children's literature authors using this tool released
two different books that both tell happy stories of enslaved cooks.
A Fine Dessert by Emily Jenkins, published by Schwartz & Wade,
and *A Birthday Cake for George Washington* by Ramin Ganeshram,
published by Scholastic, both depicted happy Black cooks joyfully
making sweets for their enslavers. An illustration from *A Birthday
Cake for George Washington* portrays six smiling, animated, intergen-
erational African Americans prepping, cooking, and serving a huge
feast. A toddler is gleefully lifting a rag in one hand while swinging
an overflowing bucket of bubbly mop water, so thrilled to be cleaning
the floor for the upcoming festivities to which he would receive no

invitation. A little girl, smiling eyes widened with anticipation, arms eagerly held up, takes in the delicious smell of the baking dessert wafting from the kitchen, a cake from which she would be offered no slice. The book centers on an enslaved chef named Hercules who attempts to make the birthday cake, but misadventure ensues when he finds there is no sugar in the house.

While slavery is depicted more subtly in A Fine Dessert, an enslaved mother and daughter still are seen smiling as they prepare a blackberry dish. After they serve the dessert to "the master and his family," they hide in a closet, kneeling in the dark to furtively lick the bowl. Rather than explain to the reader why the little girl has to work and hide, the text states "Mmmmm. Mmmmm. Mmmmm. What a fine dessert!" By representing the small joys Black people created for themselves absent the abuse, brutality, and cruelty of White enslavers, these books sell the story that the institution of slavery was Not That Bad.

The public reaction to the Not That Bad tool depicted in these books called atention to what was left out of the actual reality of slavery. Online backlash from parents and progressive education organizations was swift when the hashtag #SlaveryWithASmile started trending and think pieces circulated online about these books.[19] A coalition of #BlackLivesMatter activists, school librarians, and social justice groups circulated a petition that went viral demanding that Scholastic and the Children's Book Council "Stop promoting Racist, 'Happy Slave' Book to Children." Two prominent trade journals cautioned against the Scholastic book: the School Library Journal called it "highly problematic" and Kirkus Reviews expressed that it had "an incomplete, even dishonest treatment of slavery." After facing the online backlash, the author of A Fine Dessert apologized and donated her profits to the We Need Diverse Books campaign.

Scholastic recalled *A Birthday Cake for George Washington*, explaining, "We believe that, without more historical background on the evils of slavery than this book for younger children can provide, the book may give a false impression of the reality of the lives of slaves and therefore should be withdrawn."[20]

The Not That Bad tool is present in textbooks as well. In 2018, parent Eileen Curtright tweeted a photo from her daughter's Prentice Hall textbook that claimed:

> But the "peculiar institution," as Southerners came to call it, like all human institutions should not be oversimplified. While there were cruel masters who maimed or even killed their slaves (although killing and maiming were against the law in every state), there were also kind and generous owners. The institution was as complex as the people involved. Though most slaves were whipped at some point in their lives, a few never felt the lash. Nor did all slaves work in the fields, some were house servants or skilled artisans. Many may not have even been terribly unhappy with their lot, for they knew no other.[21]

By teaching students that enslaved people were too ignorant to be "terribly unhappy" and that there were "kind and generous owners," teachers are actively perpetuating the inaccurate idea that racism is Not That Bad for most people.

In a 2014 study, history education researchers John H. Bickford and Cynthia W. Rich examined over forty children's books about slavery and highlighted a plethora of ways that the narratives, like the examples above, distort its inhumanity. They highlight tactics used in literature such as heroification, omission, and exceptionalism—often resulting in happy endings of American progress.[22] As they explain, "To be blunt, a Holocaust story likely cannot be told without someone making someone die. A story about American slavery cannot likely be told without some violence, family separation, and little hope for freedom. . . . In short, such brutalities cannot be eliminated from the story while maintaining historicity."[23]

Teachers may be selecting books that tell a happy story in an attempt to be developmentally appropriate and to avoid traumatizing students. However, historian Blair Imani contends that if children who are BIPOC are old enough to experience racism, then it should therefore follow that White children are old enough to learn about it. As long as students who are BIPOC remain targets of racism, attempts to whitewash history do not protect children of Color; rather, they protect Whiteness. White supremacy requires this lack of historicity in order to falsely maintain the dominant narrative of Whiteness as good and innocent. Ohio State University historian Hasan Kwame Jeffries explained in a report on the way teachers misrepresent slavery: "Although we teach them that slavery happened, we fail to provide the detail or historical context they need to make sense of its origin, evolution, demise and legacy. . . . And in some cases, we minimize slavery's significance so much that we render its impact—on people and on the nation—inconsequential."[24] By creating or using premade curricula that convinces students that slavery was Not That Bad, teachers protect White innocence at the expense of Black resistance.

By claiming that historical racism is Not That Bad, teachers also imply that past oppression should have no consequence on the current status quo—in turn telling students that everything is now equal. This messaging has been shown to have negative consequences for students experiencing inequality. When students are socialized to believe that things are fair but then experience discrimination, they can't look to the system for blame—instead, they fault themselves. A 2017 study by Erin B. Godfrey, Carlos E. Santos, and Esther Burson found that "traditionally marginalized youth who grew up believing in the American ideal that hard work and perseverance naturally lead to success show a decline in self-esteem and an increase in risky behaviors during their middle-school years."[25] The findings from this study indicate that the use of tools such as Not That Bad that paint a false narrative of equality undermine the well-being of marginalized youth.

CURRICULAR TOOL OF WHITENESS: ALL THINGS BEING EQUAL

In order to maintain racial hierarchies, Whiteness requires us to buy into the false narrative that all things are equal. To admit that historical oppression has consequences on today's racial inequality would require conversations and actions such as affirmative action, reparations, and other equalizing measures that those who benefit from current arrangements aggressively resist. The tool of All Things Being Equal skews reality by collapsing the complexity of history in order to present, as Fox News would say, a "fair and balanced" perspective. When using this tool, teachers dismiss context, power, motivation, or outcomes by pretending that apples and oranges are the same fruit.

In the classroom, this tool looks similar to teaching through multiple perspectives, a popular strategy in multicultural education that encourages students to see situations from several sides. However, in contrast, when teachers use this tool, they are attempting to create a false equivalency and a seemingly neutral, even playing field, as if all sides have equal weight and circumstances. When subjected to this tool, students come to think that all opinions are equally valid, allowing for anyone to claim "fake news" if they disagree with a particular perspective. Two teacher-created worksheets from 2018 demonstrate the All Things Being Equal tool.

The first example was posted online by Roberto Livar, the father of Manú, an eighth grader in San Antonio, Texas.²⁶ It was a work-sheet titled "Slavery: A Balanced View" with a blank chart in which students were expected to list examples of both negative *and positive* aspects of slavery. In his post, Mr. Livar asked, "What the hell is this revisionist history lesson trying to achieve here!?!?"²⁷ The second worksheet was posted on Facebook by Trameka Brown-Berry, a mother in Milwaukee, Wisconsin.²⁸ The worksheet asked students to "Give 3 'good' reasons for slavery and 3 bad reasons. Make notes and then put them in complete sentences on a separate sheet to prepare for making an argument." There were blank spaces under the directions marked "Good" and "Bad." Next to the photo of the assignment, she asked, "Does anyone else find my 4th grader's homework offensive?" Over two thousand respondents found it to be so.²⁹

Both of these 2018 examples focused on the study of enslavement, the topic that is most heavily represented in curricular Tools of Whiteness, and both asked students to identify good/positive aspects of slavery. By using the tool All Sides Being Equal, these teachers created curricula that set up the false idea that one of the biggest atrocities in history can be casually debated as if both sides were equal. In addition to the moral reprehensibility of this tool, it also denies any emotional anguish that it might create for students, particularly Black students, to argue for the "goodness" of enslavement.

To successfully complete these assignments, students were expected to fill out attributes on both sides. Fortunately, the children whose parents posted the assignments rejected this indoctrination and called out the teachers for trying to turn them into slavery apologists. Manú, the student in the first example, refused to provide good reasons for slavery, writing "N/A" in that column. In the "negative" column, he responded with bullet points: "forced strenuous labor, rape, forced religion, forced sex between slaves, stolen culture, no payment, occasional torture, hardly were fed, if not being physically abused, they were verbally abused." He explained his response to receiving this assignment: "When I first read it, I thought it was B.S." Manú went on to explain that the teacher told them to respond using the textbook as well as "the stuff that we could think of off the top of our head."[30] What exactly did this teacher imagine was in their students' heads?

In the second example, fourth-grader Jerome answered: "Good? I feel there is no good reason for slavery. That's why I did not write it. BAD: Biting them. Splitting them up from family members, making them do your chores and work when it's your job to do that, and punishing them, and I am proud to be black because we are strong and brave." While it is incredibly heartening to see these young people clap back at their teachers, it is not the responsibility of students of Color to hold educators accountable for their racist curriculum.

We saw the All Sides Being Equal tool of creating false equivalents used by the forty-fifth president of the United States after the Unite the Right rally on April 11, 2017, during which White supremacists, Proud Boys, neo-Nazis, and other members of the alt-right marched with tiki torches in Charlottesville, shouting, "Jews will not replace us!" The next day, a member of this group plowed his car into counter-protesters, resulting in dozens of injuries and the death of a young White woman named Heather Heyer. Donald Trump commented on the incident, and instead of expressing condemnation for the murder, he claimed that there were "very fine people on both sides." When a reporter asked if he was equating the moral plane of the counter-protestors with that of the White supremacists, he responded:

> Yes, I think there's blame on both sides. If you look at both sides—I think there's blame on both sides. But you had a lot of people in that group [alt-right] that were there to innocently protest and very

legally protest, because you know, I don't know if you know, but they had a permit. The other group [the counter-protestors] didn't have a permit. So I only tell you this: there are two sides to a story.[31]

Trump equated two "wrongdoings": (1) protesting without a permit and (2) first-degree murder. This tactic skews the reality of the "two sides of the story" while wrongly leaving blame up for debate. The tool of equating two unequal events allows him to keep significant points out of the conversation and chalk up people's outrage to a difference of opinion, or "fake news."

The All Things Being Equal tool is appealing for many teachers because they often feel pressured to present an unbiased perspective, which they equate with not taking a stance or not assigning blame. As a teacher educator, my students often raise the concern of teacher objectivity, having been socialized to believe that classrooms should be apolitical places of knowledge transmission. Without fail, this concern always comes up in a class I lead on complicating the narrative of Christopher Columbus in elementary classrooms. Using Rethinking Schools' classic trial activity from *Rethinking Columbus*, participants explore who is guilty for the crimes against the Taino Indians by examining primary documents.[32] While the role-play asks students to consider multiple perspectives, the activity concludes by assigning blame—the key piece missing in the All Things Being Equal tool.

After the activity, we engage in a discussion of how the teachers will now teach Columbus to their students. Preservice teachers are often hesitant to stray from the traditional "Columbus sailed the Ocean Blue" version. They fear the backlash from imaginary parents who, when pressed, they realize they have pictured as White. They see moving from the official version as potential "indoctrination" but don't recognize that teaching the "*Niña, Pinta,* and *Santa María*" version is biased as well—that it is teaching the glory of imperialism.

Somehow, they don't fear a corresponding potential backlash from Indigenous parents, demonstrating the power that even non-present, imaginary Whiteness has on teachers' decision-making. The problem with the All Things Being Equal tool is not the examination of multiple perspectives or viewpoints, it's the false pretense that both sides are coming to the table from the same place.

Not surprisingly, this tool is generally reserved for when people of Color are targets of oppression. When White people are the primary perceived victims of atrocities, such as in the September 11th attacks, students are typically taught that evildoers perpetrated the violence. As Trameka Brown-Berry, the mother of fourth-grader Jerome, commented about the assignment asking her child to identify "three good reasons for slavery": "You wouldn't ask someone to list three good reasons for rape or three good reasons for the Holocaust."[33] So why is it deemed acceptable to ask students to use this line of reasoning when thinking of slavery or colonization? Again, the insidious reach of Whiteness is at play.

CURRICULAR TOOL OF WHITENESS: WHITE GAZE

Another way that Whiteness is maintained is by masking itself and attempting to collapse everyone into seeing the world through a particular perspective—the perspective of White people. Teachers achieve this through the use of a tool that Toni Morrison referred to as the White Gaze.[34] The White Gaze is set up to view people of Color, particularly Black people, through the lens of Whiteness, and it ultimately "traps black people in white imaginations."[35] With this tool, teachers use curricula that are written either explicitly or implicitly from a White perspective, asking all students to develop White sensibilities. This White Gaze tool teaches students to think like those in power, in turn preparing students to empathize with oppressors rather than those marginalized by power. This tool also trains students to problem solve to maintain inequality rather than teaching them how to dismantle it. Take the following two instances, which, in keeping with previous examples, distort the interwoven history of settler colonialism and enslavement.

The first example was an assignment that I initially saw on a fellow academic's Facebook page. It read:

Poster Assignment

You are a wealthy Southern plantation owner who had several slaves escape and head to the North. This is severely hurting your profits. Make a poster advertising for slave catchers to go find your runaway slaves. Be persuasive, make your poster stand out, and be sure to put in an incentive.

Things to remember:

Who is your audience?

What will they receive if they return with slaves?

Where will they need to travel?

When do they have to return? Is there a time limit?

Why should they do this job? Will you pay them? How much?

While I don't have information about this assignment, since it was posted without identifying information, the following diary-writing exercise was assigned in an elementary school in Edmunds, Washington. This assignment went viral after the mother of Blaine Gallagher, a Native American student of the Klamath Tribe, saw her eleven-year-old's homework. While assigned in 2018, it came from a supplemental curriculum originally published in 1971.[36]

Diary Situation 2

Since your ships' first landing in the New World, you have had constant contact with various Indian tribes. The first Indians were generally friendly. They often were very helpful. They came to your aid during that first winter. Without them, you probably would not have survived. You have welcomed them into your homes and have often shared your meals, your good times, and your sorrows.

Now tragedy has struck. Last Friday a well-organized Indian attack was launched across your colony. Several dozen colonists—men, women, and children—were slaughtered with their own guns. Many of these colonists were killed at their dinner table as they shared their meal with their "friends." This attack came as a total surprise and shock.

Write a diary account of the attack.

1. Explain exactly what happened as you viewed it.
2. Express your conflicting feelings toward the Indians.
3. Include in your account some of your past experiences with the Indians and your plans for how you will deal with them in the future.
4. Strive for verisimilitude. This word means "the quality of seeming real." To make your descriptions real, use descriptive words which create pictures in your reader's mind.

These two assignments exemplify the White Gaze tool. The teachers who used the tool forced students to take on a role—the first as a wealthy Southern plantation owner and the second as a colonist in the New World. While neither explicitly tells the student they should imagine themselves as White, a White identity is assumed in both these roles. Both assignments view Black and Indigenous people as the "White man's burden," requiring students to problem solve in order to "deal" with enslaved Africans who are ruining their "profit" by running away from slavery or to handle Native people who are launching a "shocking" attack for no apparent reason. This requires students to learn how to maintain oppression by either scheming to protect profits by catching troublemaking slaves or dealing with those violent Indians who have hurt their feelings. Both distort the brutality of enslavement and colonization, positioning White people as the victims under those systems.

A similar White Gaze assignment was posted to Facebook in December 2019 from a fifth-grade social studies class in Missouri.

> You own a plantation or farm and therefore need more workers. You begin to get involved in the slave trade industry and have slaves work on your farm. Your product to trade is slaves. Set your price for a slave_____. These could be worth a lot. You can trade for any items you'd like.

According to the school, this assignment was part of an activity that had "attempted to address market practices." The district justified the assignment, claiming, "Students were learning about having goods, needing goods and obtaining goods and how that influenced early settlement in America."[37] The activity was a role-play in which students were assigned a variety of roles, including slave owner. A biracial student, who was given this role, showed his completed worksheet to his mother, Angie Walker, who posted it online. Also an elementary teacher, Ms. Walker expressed, "For me, for my biracial son to come home, and to see '$5 for two slaves,' I was shocked." Her son told her that the assignment was meant to be "a game" to see which student could amass the most wealth through free trade. "First of all, the slave trade industry is never a game," Walker denounced. "The teacher could have gotten the lesson across perfectly fine without using slavery. It could have been a teachable moment, and things like this in 2019 should not be occurring. We can all learn from this and do better." Ms. Walker calls attention to the emotional impact the White Gaze tool has on Black students, as well as the disturbing use of the Not That Bad tool that turns slavery into a casual game.

This dehumanizing tool forces children of Color to develop the White Gaze by going outside themselves to see their own people as problems and to empathize with, identify with, and think like the very people responsible for their oppression. Assignments shaped by the White Gaze force children who are BIPOC to see themselves through the violent and deficit lens of Whiteness. As Blaine, the only Native student in the class that received the diary assignment, said, "It was upsetting. I didn't want to read it because it told me about slaughtering by my own people."[38]

Fortunately, Blaine was able to identify the problem with being asked to see his people through the eyes of his oppressors, but not all students are able to avoid this racial internalization. In such cases, the White Gaze tool puts a psychological burden on students who are BIPOC, potentially jeopardizing their academic success when confronted with such assignments. Take for example a question on a Massachusetts Comprehensive Assessment System (MCAS) exam based on Colson Whitehead's 2016 novel, *The Underground Railroad.* During this high-stakes exam, tenth graders from across the state were confronted with a passage that required them to identify with the perspective of a character named Ethel, a racist White Southern woman, in order to correctly answer the question.[39] The vice president of the Massachusetts Teachers Association reported how disturbed students were by the question: "They really felt like they were being asked to basically write creative racist thoughts and put them into words for this character. . . . This seemed like a disturbing thing to ask students—especially students of color—to do."[40]

While White students might be able to answer this question and move on, Black students are forced to experience the racial trauma of thinking about themselves through a White racist lens in order to achieve academically on a test that has implications for their future. In what ways does this take them out of the testing mindset and impact their psychological well-being and academic success? Thanks to public uproar and demands from the Massachusetts Teachers Association, the Boston Teachers Union, the American Federation of Teachers Massachusetts, the Massachusetts Education Justice Alliance, and the New England Area Conference of the NAACP, this question was removed.[41] This situation begs the question: How many other assignments like this have been created by the tool of White Gaze that have been left unaddressed?

For White children, this tool reinforces mainstream ideology about racial superiority. It socializes White children to see themselves as the ones in power and to develop paternalistic mindsets, strategies, and policies to interact with and ultimately control BIPOC. This 2019 example from a school outside Chicago demonstrates the potential outcome when White students internalize these messages. A White high school student took a picture of his Black classmate. He posted the photo on Craigslist with the headline, "Slave for Sale." The White student described his peer as a "hardworkin thick n—— slave."[42] Someone might try to assign blame for this ignorance to the single student himself or even ask where someone could learn such behavior. By enticing students into the White Gaze through curriculum, schools should not be surprised when children internalize these messages and act accordingly.

While the White student in this example used the White Gaze tool to internalize racial superiority, this tool also results in children of Color trying to avoid their identities because of the violence perpetuated upon them. An article in *The Guardian* cited how children are responding to growing racial hate crimes in the UK. The piece reported an increase in students of Color attempting to change their appearances to look more White as a way to avoid this racist bullying. As one eleven-year-old Chinese girl lamented, "I hate the way I look so much, I think if I looked different everyone would stop being mean to me and I'd fit in." A ten-year-old stated, "I've tried to make my face whiter before using makeup so that I can fit in."[43] Rather than being able to recognize the perpetrators of the bullying as racist, these children are heartbreakingly internalizing the pressure of the White Gaze tool by attempting to fit in to White standards of beauty.

CURRICULAR TOOL OF WHITENESS: EMBEDDED STEREOTYPES

Similar to the White Gaze, White supremacy benefits when people of Color are dehumanized and stereotyped. Teachers can consciously or unconsciously enact Whiteness by using the Embedded Stereotype tool. This tool relies on a hidden curriculum to socialize students to develop racial stereotypes by camouflaging them in lessons on unrelated academic skills—for example, math or literacy. The teacher may be teaching a lesson that appears to be on a neutral skill, like addition or rhyming, but the content relies on mainstream or historical stereotypes. In other words, the lesson isn't about the offending stereotype—the teaching of the stereotype is a secondary effect.

An egregious example of the Embedded Stereotype tool came from a reading series called *Little Books* from Reading Horizons, a curriculum purchased in 2015 for $1.2 million by the Minneapolis Public School District.[44] One *Little Book* page is an illustration of an African girl running out of a hut in a simple orange dress. The title of this story is "Lazy Lucy." The other page shows a dark-skinned, smiling runner, arms lifted in triumph. The text reads:

> People in Kenya are very active in sports. They play rugby and soccer. They also like boxing. Most people are aware that Kenyans are able to run very fast. They can run for a long time. Kenyans have won many races. Some Kenyans run with bare feet! As you can tell, Kenya is a pretty great place.[45]

The district purchased this curriculum filled with essentializing stereotypes as part of its Acceleration 2020 initiative, specifically aimed at closing the "performance gap between white students and students of color." In keeping with how this tool functions, the content about Kenyans being lazy or running fast wasn't the goal of the lesson; literacy development using decoding skills was the intended lesson objective. Socializing students to develop stereotypical thinking that maintains racial hierarchies was the embedded curriculum of racism.

While the above examples are from literacy curriculum, the Embedded Stereotypes tool shows up frequently in mathematic lessons as well. The following examples demonstrate the tool in use when teachers integrate race into math problems.

Mathematics Example 1

The master needed 192 slaves to work on the plantation in the cotton fields. The fields could fill 75 bags of cotton. Only 96 slaves were able to pick cotton for that day. The missus needed them in the Big House to prepare for the Annual Picnic. How many more slaves are needed in the cotton fields?

Note: Follow the three reads protocol to *identify what you understand*, what you know, your plan and how to solve.

Picture (Show your work)[46]

Mathematics Example 2

If Frederick got two beatings per day, how many beatings did he get in 1 week? 2 weeks?

Each tree had 56 oranges. If 8 slaves pick them equally, then how much would each slave pick?

Frederick had 6 baskets filled with cotton. If each basket held 5 pounds, how many pounds did he have all together?[47]

Mathematics Example 3

In a slave ship, there can be 3,799 slaves. One day, the slaves took over the ship. 1,897 are dead. How many slaves are alive?

One slave got whipped five times a day. How many times did he get whipped in a month (31 days)? Another slave got whipped nine times a day. How many times did he get whipped in a month? How many times did the two slaves get whipped together in one month?[48]

These three assignments are explicitly mathematics problems, but implicitly they reduce Black people to the role of slaves who are either working for master and missus or are being violently beaten, whipped, or killed. Some might argue that these teachers were trying to strengthen their curriculum by integrating social studies content into their mathematical lessons. However, their problematic racial ideology was revealed through their application of the tool of Embedded Stereotypes.

Another horrific example of the Embedded Stereotype tool comes from a Burns Middle School teacher in Alabama, who passed out a quiz that included these questions:

- Leroy has 2 ounces of cocaine. If he sells an 8 ball to Antonio for $320 and 2 grams to Juan for $85 per gram, what is the street value of the rest of his hold?

- Pedro got 6 years for murder. He also got $10,000 for the hit. If his common law wife spends $100 of his hit money per month, how much money will be left when he gets out?

- Tyrone knocked up 4 girls in the gang. There are 20 girls in his gang. What is the exact percentage of girls Tyrone knocked up?

▪ Marvin steals Juan's skateboard. As Marvin skates away
at 15 mph, Juan loads his 357 Magnum. If it takes Juan
20 seconds to load his piece, how far away will Marvin
be when he gets whacked?[49]

This quiz, floating around online as a piece of "satire" for over a
decade, had already caused teachers in California, Texas, and New
Mexico to be disciplined.[50] In the Alabama case, the teacher told the
students that it was *not* meant as a joke and they had to complete
it and turn it in.[51] Perhaps some teachers are using this tool in an
attempt to be "down" or culturally relevant, but because their understandings of race are rife with deficit thinking, the result is reproducing deeply problematic stereotypes. In writing about this specific
assignment, mathematics scholars Julius Davis and Christopher C.
Jett explain, "These kinds of examples . . . contribute to stereotypical, deficit constructions of Black people and reflect what Blackness
often means in the White imagination."[52]

While the stereotypes in the prior examples are explicitly stated,
the following examples illustrate how the Embedded Stereotype tool
can also covertly promote the socialization of implicit bias. Observed
in children as young as six years old, implicit bias is the unconscious,
involuntary racist attitude that individuals have about groups outside of their personal experience.[53] When teachers use curricula that
embed false, negative assumptions about different groups, this socializes students to develop implicit bias and negative associations from
an early age. The materials teachers create using this tool do not
explicitly focus on racist content; rather, they cunningly reinforce
racism through a more hidden curriculum.[54]

An example of this tool is a worksheet posted online by Aqkhira
S-Aungkh, who found it in a K–1 vocabulary workbook published in
2009 by Carson Dellosa.[55] The assignment had four children with

no facial expressions with a traced emotion word underneath each child. The instructions were to trace the word and then to draw the child's face to match the feeling. Of the four children, two were White and two were Black. The White girl, wearing a party hat, is "happy," and the White boy, wearing a first-place ribbon, is "proud." In contrast, the Black boy, who has a popped balloon, is "sad," and the Black girl, whose dog ate her homework, is "angry." This worksheet, aimed at teaching five-year-olds how to name their feelings, taught an additional hidden lesson in assigning racialized emotions that reinforce existing stereotypes such as that of the angry Black woman and that of White men as the most advanced.

Aqkhira S-Aungkh captioned the photo, "It's the subtle, subliminal messages that we have to watch out for. Those images that seep into our children's sub conscience and derail their confidence. Not on my watch! Not my brilliant babies!"[56] Here S-Aungkh recognizes and uncovers the tool of Embedded Stereotypes. The post was picked up by a number of media outlets, prompting the publisher to apologize: "It has been brought to our attention that our *Homework Helpers Vocabulary Development Workbook* features an occurrence of implied racism."[57] While the embedded racism was addressed in this example, in many assignments, it goes unnoticed and is therefore easily internalized by students.

Another example, while not a piece of classroom curriculum, is an instructional poster called "Be Cool, Follow the Rules," put out in 2014 by the American Red Cross as part of a safe swimming campaign.[58] It portrays a number of diverse children engaged in poolside activities labeled as either "cool" or "not cool." The two characters engaged in "cool" activities are White, while four out of the five characters engaging in dangerous or violent activities identified with "not cool" arrows are children of Color. Because the "cool" children are White and the "not cool" children are people of Color, this tool

of Embedded Stereotypes is sending racialized messages of validation and inferiority. Fortunately, people noticed this embedded racism and pushed back. Swimmer Margaret Sawyer saw the poster at a
few local pools, complained about the racist portrayal, and posted it
online. In an article in the *Washington Post* about the poster, Ebony
Rosemond, who heads an organization called Black Kids Swim, connected the poster to both historical and current lack of swimming
resources for Black children and stated, "The current state of affairs
is unfortunate, and images like the one created and circulated by the
Red Cross make things worse." Rosemond continued, "In connection with the lack of images showing African Americans excelling
in swimming, the poster doesn't make you feel welcome—it suggests
to a Black child that you're not welcome here."[59]

The viral backlash prompted the American Red Cross to apologize and remove the poster. While a kindergartener is likely unaware
of the racist legacy of segregated swimming pools, the American Red
Cross poster still teaches them the lesson that pools are not cool for
Black children. As with other instances of the Embedded Stereotype
tool, these visuals educate generations that might not know the history behind these images to still hold the same stereotypical beliefs as
generations before. The workbook and the poster exemplify implicitly Embedded Stereotypes—the lessons are explicitly on safety and
feelings, but the images reinforce racialized assignments of value and
emotions. In concert, the wide range of assignments in this tool work
powerfully to inculcate students into learning mainstream stereotypes
while camouflaging them within lessons on unrelated academic skills.

CURRICULAR TOOL OF WHITENESS: RACIST REPRODUCTION

Over the last decade, no other tool has been responsible for more examples of viral curriculum than the Racist Reproduction tool. In my
research, I came across over twenty viral examples in which teachers

forced Black children to role-play slaves in reenactments of different aspects of enslavement. While the other tools work to shape students' ideology so that they think in ways that keep racial hierarchies in place, teachers using the Racist Reproduction tool provide actual practice in reenacting historical racism through role-plays, skits, games, and simulations.

One example is from 2018 in Westchester, New York, in which a White fifth-grade teacher stood in front of her class and asked her students, "Who is Black?" She then made the Black children who raised their hands line up outside in the hallway. She "pretended to place them in shackles" and then brought them back inside the classroom, where she lined them up against the wall. Playing the role of slave auctioneer, she instructed the White students to bid on them.[60]

The Racist Reproduction tool is particularly insidious because it gives teachers the opportunity to appear to be educating students about racism, which is a good thing, while in actuality they re-create racial hierarchies in ways that traumatize Black children. In other words, they are enacting racism in the name of anti-racism. The prevalence of this tool is astounding—the headlines below are from 2019 alone:

"Teacher on Leave and Under Investigation; Parents Claim Teacher Held 'Mock Slave Auction'" (Watertown, NY)

"5th Grade Teacher Tells White Students to Bid on Black Classmates in Mock Slave Auction" (Bronxville, NY)

"Wisconsin Teacher Reportedly Asks 7th Graders to Create 'Slave Games'" (Shorewood, WI)

"'Monopoly-Like' Slavery Game Played by Fourth-Grade NC Class Outrages African-American Grandmother" (Wilmington, NC)

"For Black History Month, This Loudoun County Elementary School Played a Runaway Slave 'Game' in Gym Class" (Brambleton, VA)

"Indiana Middle School Cancels 'Slave Ship' Role-Play Lesson After Parents Raise Concerns" (Russiaville, IN)

"South Carolina Mom Outraged After Kids Told to Pick Cotton, Sing Slave Song as 'Game'" (Rock Hill, SC) [61]

The sheer number of times this Racist Reproduction happens begs the question: What is it about enslavement that makes this the topic teachers are most committed to reenacting? Historian Carol Anderson, in her seminal book *White Rage*, demonstrates that for every advancement made by African Americans in the United States, White people have relentlessly pushed back against these hard-fought gains.[62] Because slavery has been legally abolished, perhaps White teachers are enacting this White rage by using their limited classroom power to force students into explicitly anti-Black oppression under the pretense of learning.

While the use of this tool is prevalent, so, too, is the backlash by those who see the racist implications of these activities. It is no surprise that the majority of the headlines charted above center the outrage of Black families. Mother Nicole Dayes described a mock slave auction that her ten-year-old son's teacher in Watertown engaged in:

He and another African American child were put up in the middle of the class and told they were now slaves. The teacher then started the "bidding." . . . After the winning bid was placed, my son was then told how slaves would take the slave owners' last name and what he was to call the slave owner by. Then my son and the other "slave" were instructed to call the Caucasian child by "master" and the child's last name.[63]

In South Carolina, parents were outraged when fifth graders were brought on a field trip to a cotton field. With no explanation of slavery or the significance of forced labor, they were instructed to play a "game" in which they had to race to pick cotton while singing the following song lyrics: "I like it when you fill the sack. I like it when you don't talk back. Make money for me."[64] By turning slavery into a game, the Racist Reproduction tool works in concert with the Not That Bad tool by obscuring the atrocities of enslavement.

In 2018, the Southern Poverty Law Center issued a report on the inadequacy of how slavery is taught in schools.[65] The report was highly critical of the use of these kinds of simulations, arguing that they "'can harm vulnerable children' and that the trauma of such lessons is compounded for black students." While the teachers in these examples may have been teaching about historical events, they ultimately set their students up to experience the very same conditions they were teaching about—racial hierarchies with Black students on the bottom and White students on the top. Through the Racist Reproduction tool, teachers commit educational malpractice, using their position of power to enact traumatic events that carry very real health and psychological consequences for Black students.

CURRICULUM VIOLENCE

Each of the examples in this chapter function as *curriculum violence*, a term coined by Erhabor Ighodaro, which he defines as the "deliberate manipulation of academic programming in a manner that ignores or compromises the intellectual and psychological well-being of learners."[66] This form of violence perpetuated by educators includes both the omission as well as the falsification of the history, culture, and representation of people of Color.[67] The result of this curricular violence is the socialization of racist beliefs in students and the traumatization of children of Color.

While the viral nature of current examples might make it appear that curriculum violence is something new, there is a long legacy of teachers using education as a way to transmit White supremacy. In 1933, Carter G. Woodson explained, "To handicap a student by teaching him that his black face is a curse and that the struggle to change his condition is hopeless is the worst sort of lynching. . . . This crusade [against propaganda in school] is much more important than the anti-lynching movement because there would be no lynching if it did not start in the schoolroom."[68] Here, Woodson connects curriculum to physical violence, demonstrating how both serve an explicit purpose of maintaining power and control.

In contrast to the immediate terror of murder, however, such "schoolroom lynching" serves instead as a form of *slow violence*, which "occurs gradually and out of sight, a violence of delayed destruction that is dispersed across time and space."[69] Rob Nixon explains that this kind of slow violence "is typically not viewed as violence at all . . . a different kind of violence, a violence that is neither spectacular nor instantaneous, but rather incremental and accretive."[70]

EDUCATIONAL MALPRACTICE

Like traditional notions of violence, slow violence has a tangible impact on health. A 2019 national report from American Academy of Pediatrics (AAP) explained how Black children suffer significantly from racism and named racism as a social determinant of health that "has a profound impact on the health status of children, adolescents, emerging adults, and their families." Referring to racism as a "socially transmitted disease passed down through generations," the AAP acknowledged that children who are the targets of racism have the most significant health impacts.[71]

One way that the health field measures the impact of trauma is through the Adverse Childhood Experiences score, or ACE score. An ACE score refers to the multiple factors of stress, abuse, and neglect that children can face that impact their later health outcomes. Examples include psychological, physical, and sexual abuse; exposure in the home to substance abuse, mental illness, and suicide; incarceration or violence; physical and emotional neglect; parental separation and divorce; exposure to violence outside of the home; living in unsafe neighborhoods; homelessness; bullying; discrimination based on race or ethnicity; and experience of income insecurity.[72]

According to the AAP report, when an individual is exposed to discrimination, or even anticipates discrimination, they experience stress responses including "feelings of intense fear, terror, and helplessness."[73] As a result, hormones such as cortisol flood the body, which can lead to inflammation, ultimately making the body more open to chronic diseases.[74] Health officials warn that: "When activated repeatedly or over a prolonged period of time (especially in the absence of protective factors), toxic levels of stress hormones can interrupt normal physical and mental development and can even change the brain's architecture."[75] The more ACE factors children experience, the more likely they are to be linked to some of the negative outcomes associated with high ACE scores, such as depression, suicide, poor physical health, obesity, lower educational attainment, unemployment, and poverty.[76]

Children's ACE scores are not race neutral. According to a 2016 National Survey of Children's Health (NSCH), 61 percent of Black children and 51 percent of Latinx children have experienced at least one ACE factor compared with 40 percent of White children and

23 percent of Asian children.[77] The trauma connected with health determinants is often associated with what children carry into schools from their outside lives.[78] However, these already elevated ACE scores that Black and Latinx students experience outside of school are compounded when they experience additional stressors, such as racism, inside schools.

Through curricular Tools of Whiteness, it is teachers and their curriculum that become the active source of trauma for children of Color. When students experience stress reactions to the racism exposed through #CurriculumSoWhite, it can be inferred that it will also impact "how the brain and body respond to stress, resulting in short- and long-term health impacts on achievement and mental and physical health."[79] Given that Black and Latinx children already experience more ACE factors than White children do because of an interconnected web of health determinants, curricular Tools of Whiteness re-traumatize them in classrooms that should ideally be set up to support them. Taken as a whole, then, curricular Tools of Whiteness are more than problematic assignments; rather, they are issues of serious health concerns, particularly for Black students who already have the highest ACE scores and are subjected to the most frequent racism through #CurriculumSoWhite. Teachers using Tools of Whiteness add to the ACE scores of children of Color through the racial trauma they induce by exposing their students to this kind of educational malpractice.

RESPONSE CYCLE: THE WRONG I

The life cycle of #CurriculumSoWhite appears to follow a pattern— at least as the media that reports on it would have us believe. First, a racist assignment is given to a student. The student, typically a student of Color, shares the offending assignment with a family member who recognizes the racist nature of the activity. They post it on social media, eliciting a viral response from an outraged online

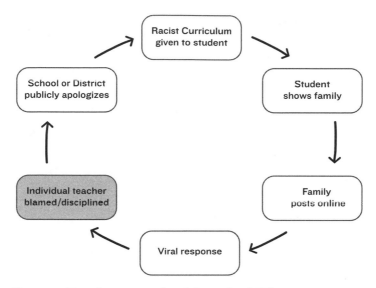

Figure 2. *Typical response cycle to #CurriculumSoWhite*

community. In a defensive move, the school or school district suspends, disciplines, or removes the teacher and offers a public apology. Things settle down. Until it happens again.

As I was writing this chapter, this same response cycle was once again in the news. Following the typical pattern, a teacher in Freeport, New York, gave her eighth graders an assignment to create captions for black-and-white photographs from after the Civil War of Black sharecroppers working in a field. Instead of focusing on the import of these rarely seen primary documents from the era, the teacher instructed students to "make it funny," adding, "Don't bore me."[80] A student told her grandmother about the assignment, who posted it on her Facebook page where it went viral. The image of the completed worksheet showed how students resisted the racism of this assignment, filling it out with phrases such as "I HATE THIS," "#BlackGirlMagic," and "Us Black people need to GET OUT!"

The next day, the teacher offered an apology, recognizing that she must "work hard to rebuild trust from my students, colleagues, and the community." The superintendent issued a public statement claiming, "Our investigation has determined that this lesson was poorly conceived and executed . . . Aside from the fact that this is a poor lesson, it is an insensitive trivialization of a deeply painful era for African Americans in this country, and it is unacceptable." While this accountability and apology are important, this typical response cycle is incapable of interrupting the ongoing onslaught of #CurriculumSoWhite. Part of the reason goes back to the Four I's of Oppression and Advantage: this response isolates only one of the I's and operates solely on the interpersonal level by assigning blame to an individual "racist" teacher, treating them like a bad apple that, if isolated and dealt with, will make the problem go away.

The truth is that a more complicated response is required. While there does need to be a change in the racial understandings of individual teachers, it cannot be done in a piecemeal, case-by-case manner after the offending curriculum has done its damage. In order to effectively mitigate curricular Tools of Whiteness, all Four I's of Oppression and Advantage—interpersonal, ideological, institutional, and internalized—must be addressed. Understanding how the Four I's are implicated in the problem also points us toward a solution. There must be an institutional attempt to transform the interpersonal and internalized ideology of educators.

Teacher education is one such institution that has the capacity to disrupt the racial ideology of large numbers of teachers before they enter the field poised to cause damage. The following chapter digs deeper into how focusing teacher education on racial literacy can transform the deeply held racial beliefs of White teachers and how that impacts their curricular choices. By understanding the relationship between teachers' ideology and curriculum, the response cycle can move from the interpersonal level to working at the institutional level to admit, transform, and graduate teachers who recognize Whiteness and actively seek to interrupt it.

CHAPTER 2

THE ICEBERG: RACIAL IDEOLOGY AND CURRICULUM

To not commit yourself actively to an anti-racist lifestyle is,
in fact, a default to racism. A default setting is the way a system
is designed to function automatically without interference from
users. The system relies on complacency to exist. Our country
is literally on a default setting to racism.

—DIANA, TEACHER

Understanding how curricular Tools of Whiteness operate is critical, but the tools cannot be divorced from the educators who employ them. What teachers choose to teach represents their individual ways of thinking about race, which have been influenced by broader racial ideologies. As they enact this ideology through curricular Tools of Whiteness, teachers transfer these individual forms of racism in ways that have institutional impact on students. Given that *Reading, Writing, and Racism* draws attention to how teachers' racial ideology affects what they choose to teach, this chapter examines what teachers believe about race and how this shows up in their curriculum.

Most of the teachers creating or enacting racialized curricular violence are not tiki torch–carrying White nationalists.[1] Rather, many of them may very well be doing what they believe is best for their students, but because they have not had the opportunity to

63

examine their own ideas about race, they make problematic choices when deciding what to teach.

When teachers, particularly White teachers, have the opportunity to examine their racial ideology, the way in which they respond to the inquiry shapes their choice to either use Tools of Whiteness or pivot toward racial justice. It is in the response to examination of their ideology that change is possible. If teachers are resistant, they will likely use the tools to protect their socialized beliefs about racial hierarchies, passing their ideology on to students. However, if they are willing to be open to examining their beliefs, to question how this influences what they do in the classroom, and to transform their practice, there is hope for change. For future teachers, the capacity to take these steps of self-reflection are how an anti-racist curriculum can be built. This chapter shows the pathway from teachers' ideological roots to the curriculum they ultimately teach, mitigated by how they respond to exposure to anti-racist teacher education.

CASE STUDIES

In this chapter, I will introduce four White teachers, using pseudonyms for all. They are each former students of mine spanning across my career of preparing educators. As my students, they were in courses that aimed to prepare them for urban teaching, to help them understand their own racial identity, to develop an analysis of institutional racism, to teach them the foundations of curriculum design, and to support them in designing and implementing a social justice interdisciplinary unit. In writing their cases, I reviewed papers they wrote, including racial autobiographies about the role that race has played throughout their lives, written reflections on critical professional development that they participated in throughout their programs, and reflective papers in which they were specifically asked to consider their journey in terms of new understandings about race.

My goal for each of the cases is to demonstrate how curriculum is simply the tip of the iceberg; it is what is made visible about teachers' understandings of race. Lying beneath the surface is the foundational structure of their racial ideology. It is these underlying beliefs that are revealed through the way race is addressed through their curriculum. This chapter therefore examines the relationship between these teachers' ideologies and the curricula they design and teach. The ultimate purpose of this analysis is to argue that teacher education must attend to transforming foundational beliefs rather than tinkering with curriculum, which is what typically happens through methods and curriculum design courses. The cases are organized and presented by how the individual teachers responded to teacher education coursework designed to challenge racist ideology. Each case represents one of four responses along a continuum: protectionism, open-mindedness, questioning, and transformation.

CASE I: WHITE PROTECTIONISM

To demonstrate how the case studies illustrate the relationship between racial ideology and curriculum, I begin with Dawn, who was a young White first-grade teacher working toward her master's degree when she was my student. When Dawn was a five-year-old child, a hate crime occurred in her hometown that gained national notoriety. Three Black men stopped into a restaurant after their car broke down in her predominately Italian American neighborhood. A group of ten White teenagers then beat them and pursued them through the neighborhood. They chased one of the Black men onto a local freeway, where he was struck by a car and killed. Rather than empathizing with the victims of this hate crime, Dawn's family was outraged by the Black protesters mobilizing after the event who she felt "invaded" what she described as a quiet, idyllic neighborhood. They saw the protestors as the source of conflict rather than the violence of the White teenagers. She described the time: "I remem-ber my mom being scared. Like saying that Black people were going to come back and get us. . . . I had never seen this many Black people in my whole life. And I thought they were coming to get us." As a White Italian American girl, she was socialized into developing a fear of Black people that has stayed with her throughout her life. She admitted that as an adult, "when I'm walking around the neighbor-hood, or driving around the neighborhood, and I see a Black man, I'm automatically terrified."

As a result, this fear translated into strong anti-Black under-standings about race and a denial of racism. In responding to a ques-tion about how to address racism, she proclaimed, "Get over it! Like get over it! . . . You know, move on! So what, you're Black; so what, I'm White. If I get better grades in school—maybe I worked harder. You know, if I get a job, maybe I deserved it! Why does it always have to be like [whiny voice], 'Well, they're the minority, let's give it to them.' I'm done with that, it's time to start a new life."

Dawn's racial ideology, developed as a child, is akin to the idea of *reverse racism*, in which White people are framed as the victims of racism and people of Color are perceived as receiving unfair and undeserved privileges. Similar to how the curricular Tools of White-ness of No One Is to Blame and All Things Being Equal function, she does not acknowledge the negative impact that institutional or historical racism currently has on people of Color, especially Black people. She subscribes to the idea of the American meritocracy: We all exist on an equal playing field and hard work pays off. What Dawn feels is disrupting this meritocracy is that racism was overcor-rected: it was something that existed, it was solved, and now White people are the actual victims because people of Color are benefiting unfairly from unnecessary restorative measures such as affirmative action. She explained, "My brother was rejected from the university because a minority, with a 900 SAT score, was needed to fill a seat. My family believes if you work hard, you deserve the reward. You do not deserve the reward on the basis of the color of your skin." Here she revealed her strong resentment toward BIPOC, as she believed they are undeservingly stealing what presumably belongs to her and her family.

One of the course readings, Gary Howard's *We Can't Teach What We Don't Know*, introduced her to the concept of White privilege. She expressed intense anger in response: "Every time he said the word *privilege* . . . that just drove me crazy. . . . I'm White, so that means I have to pay full tuition. I don't get it! I mean, when we go to college, we have to check off what race you are, and I hate to say it but if you are African American or Hispanic—you get looked at first. . . . I mean, this really pisses me off." Dawn saw this attempt at reconciling historical racism as a direct attack on White people: "We don't have privilege anymore—they do. And they keep going back to saying, 'Well—we had a bad life in the past.' You weren't around then, ya know!" Dawn's response demonstrates her lack of openness to examining her socialized understandings of people of Color stealing from her family and community. Rather than reflecting on historical racism or White privilege, she doubles down on defending and protecting her inherent beliefs.

Many White individuals hold similar opinions about reverse racism. Because Dawn carries institutional power as an educator, there is no way to separate these racist ideas from how she conceives of history, and, therefore, her conception of social studies curriculum. Because Dawn believes that Black people are no longer negatively impacted by racism, she uses curricular Tools of Whiteness that align with this ideology when planning what to teach. In her attempt to teach her students that racism is over, she misuses a historical example of six-year-old African American Ruby Bridges, who was one of the first children to integrate an all-White elementary school in the 1960s. *The Story of Ruby Bridges*, introduced to Dawn in our course, is a popular children's book used in elementary schools to teach about the civil rights movement. Dawn claimed: "Like there were laws made and Ruby Bridges came along and she changed everything, and you know there was that teacher that said, 'Let's make a change,' and there were so many things that people did to help people to make things better." Rather than seeing this story as a legacy of racism, Dawn interpreted it as having solved racism; therefore, to her, strategies such as affirmative action or reparations were deemed unnecessary. "Now we are all going into the classroom, we are going to make things a little more better because we are becoming educated in what to do in the classroom, so I don't really think we have to say the words 'I'm sorry.'" This claim implies that now that things are "more better," anti-racist work is unnecessary. While in this example she was talking about reparations, the leap to curriculum is not far behind.

Not surprisingly, Dawn used curricular Tools of Whiteness to create curriculum that downplayed the realities of racism. In describing her goals for a mandated lesson for Martin Luther King Day, Dawn used the curricular Tools of Whiteness of No One Is To Blame along with All Things Being Equal. She recalled: "When I was talking about Martin Luther King, it was very uncomfortable. Like the kids were like, 'Oh, White people are all bad.' And I was like, 'Nooo! We're not all bad!' . . . I was thinking we shouldn't be getting into this and I was getting nervous. . . . I don't want them going home and saying we are bad people." When Dawn attempted to teach about Martin Luther King, she was confronted with what he was actually fighting against: racism. She experienced trepidation that she might be tarnishing the reputation of White people, which was clearly an area "she shouldn't be getting into."

In trying to figure out how to keep teaching history without making White people feel bad, she reveals the concerns that justified her use of tools such as Not That Bad: "I mean, you have to know about history, but I don't want all the kids to know that since we are White that we all hurt Black people." Here she reveals her true teaching objective: Protect White people and do not reveal them as the perpetrators of racism. In order to align her curriculum to this objective, she started to question the resources she had available to her. "So a lot of the books, it's about White and White and White did this to the Blacks, so I am trying to figure out ways to stop that so much, and to say the Whites did good for the Blacks and the Blacks did good for the Whites. Not that Whites did bad, Whites did bad, Whites did bad." Rather than teach the history of "Whites did bad," Dawn relied on her racial ideology to look for ways to revise the historical records, instead teaching that everyone "did good." Dawn used the tool of Not That Bad to protect her White students from potentially feeling down about themselves if they were to learn about historical racism. This perception fit with her childhood sense of being personally attacked when issues of anti-Black racism were raised, and she was nervous that her students would feel similarly.

By using multiple curricular Tools of Whiteness, Dawn is situated to transmit her ahistorical White apologist understandings of race to her elementary students by denying them the actual history of racism. Her racial ideology is aligned with tools such as Not That Bad in her attempt to teach how "Whites did good for the Blacks." She ultimately socializes her White students to maintain White supremacy by protecting White innocence and instilling a lack of understanding of how racism operates. When teachers such as Dawn are presented with the problematic textbooks seen in the last chapter, their racial ideology aligns with the racist literacies in the curriculum. This creates a seamless route for the transmission of racist ideologies as teachers unquestioningly use these textbooks, such as the one that claims enslaved Africans were just "workers" who came to America as part of patterns of immigration. By using the textbooks she is handed, Dawn can teach her first graders that "Whites did good for the Blacks" by providing "international job opportunities," never having to worry if "Whites did bad."

CASE 2: OPEN-MINDEDNESS

The second case participant, Grace, is a teacher who grew up in a segregated White town and was socialized to have a *race-evasive* ideology.[2] She reflects: "I wasn't taught to look at skin color; I was taught that we were all the same. I like to believe that I was raised open-mindedly, but now I wonder if I was raised naively. Perhaps never understanding true diversity or celebrating cultural differences was a bad thing." While she framed her upbringing as not noticing race, she simultaneously revealed that she had been holding racial stereotypes that were uncovered when she discussed the city she would be teaching in: "I thought of Newark as an impoverished neighborhood based on sex, drugs, and violence. Newark, in my eyes, was 'the ghetto,' 'the hood,' and it was a big city I lived in fear of."

However, unlike Dawn, she began to demonstrate open-mindedness in being willing to examine the source of those stereotypes: "As I began to think about my understanding of Newark and from where I have drawn these conclusions, I began to realize I only knew what other people have told me. I saw Newark through the eyes of everyone around me." Grace recognized that she had been taught these ideas, revealing that she might be open to revising them.

Grace's orientation to her teaching community did indeed shift dramatically. Her midyear reflection expressed gratitude and excitement to begin teaching in a diverse urban community, and she thrived on the exposure to new people and cultures. Although she had race-evasive roots, her open response to her new context supported her in making curricular choices that demonstrated the emerging value she placed on diversity. She expressed excitement about her new setting, saying, "[Through this program] I've been exposed to different cultures, ethnicities, families, and environments that I was never really exposed to before. I am aware of the various cultures, ethnicities, and races that surround me, and I could not be happier with where I have ended up or more excited to begin this journey in getting to meet many different people from a million different walks of life. I like to believe that I have seen enough to understand that being different is inevitable, yet it's a beautiful thing." Grace's race-evasive ideology shifted into one that was open to diversity.

In keeping with the argument of this chapter that a teacher's thinking is directly related to their adoption and creation of curriculum, Grace's new openness to diversity manifested itself in what she chose to teach. Three years into her teaching, she created and taught a unit in which she actively moved away from the White Out tool. She started the unit by having her first graders define and identify diversity in a few children's books that had various amounts of representation. The children noticed that White people, boys, and able-bodied people were overrepresented in their picture books and that people who were Black, Brown, disabled, babies, and elderly were often missing. The students then went through all the books in the classroom library and gathered data about who was represented or missing in terms of race, gender, and ability. They noted that "our library is not diverse" and that "there's too much of the same kind of people." Using grade-level mathematics, the students graphed their findings and reflected on how unrepresentative their library was and how they felt about that. Because they decided it was unfair, Grace led them in an activity to write a letter to the PTA for more inclusive books.

Grace was open to examining her preconceived race-evasive socialization and learned to value diversity. In turn, this ideology found its way directly into her curriculum, through which her students could develop the same understandings about diversity and representation that came out of her own shifted thinking. Unlike her upbringing, her students were taught to value diversity and to develop a critical lens in terms of representation—which pivoted them away from reinvesting in a belief in a White norm. Through this shift in Grace's thinking, her curriculum does not reinvest in Whiteness; instead, it breaks the cycle by providing her students a more open way of seeing the world.

What seemed to mitigate the differences between Dawn's and Grace's resulting curricula were their responses to their teacher education program's anti-racist initiatives. Rather than respond with Dawn's defensiveness, Grace was open to new ideas. Throughout her experience in the program, she learned to develop a political analysis that forced her to question her socialization and the ideas she held. She reflected: "I think it's safe to say I had a very naive perception of education, teaching, and Newark and hadn't really established a firm perspective of my own. The most valuable piece of advice I've learned from this class is to challenge others' ideas, opinions, and perspectives and create my own."

Grace's receptiveness allowed her to start to recognize the multiple perspectives inherent in diversity. "This class has helped me better understand that there are multiple sides to every story and that there may not necessarily be a right or wrong answer, but I owe it to myself to listen to all sides and challenge all sides before creating an opinion of my own." Grace's case demonstrates the role that having an open-minded stance can play in shifting racial ideology and, as a result, in creating a more critical multicultural curriculum.

CASE 3: QUESTIONING

While Dawn's response to racial justice curriculum was defensiveness and Grace's was openness, the subject of the third case, Cara, responded with questioning. A questioning stance moves past the openness of celebrating diversity to an exploration of how diversity can be experienced as oppression that impacts various groups of people in different ways. In this vein, questioning includes a willingness to engage, challenge, and disrupt power dynamics. Like Grace, Cara grew up in a privileged setting. She explained, "I grew up in a rich White town. My mom woke me up daily and made me breakfast. We sat on the front porch together while I waited for my bus." Despite this privileged background that was different from that of her students, she did not rely on a deficit lens to understand her school community. Instead, she started questioning and began to actively monitor, interrogate, and transform her thinking. She reflected on her stance: "It was only within the last few years that I have been studying and examining White privilege, societal and structural racism, and deficit thinking. I constantly am *reassessing and rethinking* [emphasis added] my actions, choices, and words relating to these topics. I started to challenge my own thinking and think about my own privilege and how I interact with the world." Cara was able to question her upbringing and shift away from the way she was socialized.

Cara went beyond the "respect for diversity" seen in Grace and moved to thinking about power by consistently reassessing her own positionality as a White woman working in a community of Color. She often worried about being a "stereotypical White teacher" or enacting White privilege in problematic ways. She worried, "As a White woman . . . my biggest fear was that the students would perceive me as a person who doesn't understand them or someone who doesn't have high expectations for them—or even worse, someone they can't relate to." She worked to negate this fear by connecting with her students as individuals and becoming a part of the school community.

In 2016, during Cara's student teaching year in Newark, New Jersey, the local news aired a story that thirty public schools in the city had high levels of lead in their water supplies. This was two years prior to the nationally recognized 2018 Newark water crisis, when it was revealed that the entire city's water supply had higher lead content than that of Flint, Michigan. At the time, the focus was exclusively on these thirty identified schools, and Cara's school was not one of them. However, the news still impacted her significantly. She pondered: "Perhaps I didn't think that something like this could possibly happen at a place where I am teaching. . . . I never had to worry about my well-being in any aspect. Now I am in a school where these are not the realities." Because she knew her school was deemed safe, she allowed the children to drink from the water fountains, yet she brought in a water bottle for herself. She started to deeply question her own response to the situation. "I am focused on my thought process. I'm asking myself, why? Things were so much easier before I learned about privilege and racism."

Cara was able to identify the way that learning about racism wasn't simply a topic or content; instead, it became a lens that changed the way she viewed the world. "Sometimes I feel like my awareness is really powerful and I am making little changes here and there. But I cannot find the answers as to why the water at [school] was not good enough for me to drink, but it was fine for the kids . . . They trust me; what do I do?" Cara's new lens prompted her to question herself, her privilege, and her response. It would follow that this new way of thinking would work its way into her teaching.

She decided to use her curriculum to teach about the lead in the water. Just as she was learning to question the world around her, the unit she developed also centered around providing students the opportunity to engage in similar inquiry. She explained, "To counterbalance my initial response, I created curriculum for myself and my students to take collective action on the topic. I wanted to do something to challenge, stir up, and break through some of the preexisting ideas and feelings around social justice in the classroom."

She decided to create a research project fueled by student-generated questions about the water crisis. Students brainstormed questions then researched everything they had identified that they wanted to learn. Students were provided accessible resources and spent time researching using laptops, newspaper, visuals, and videos while taking copious notes. Once the students gathered all their information about each question, they were able to choose how they would present their findings to other classes. The students recognized that most of the materials they were reading were written for adults, so they decided to make their own kid-friendly brochures and posters to share with others at their school.

Cara explained: "During these lessons, I have given the students the space to talk about it, get some facts, and feel that their well-being is a priority. Since I grew up in a place where I never needed to worry about issues such as environmental racism, I ended up learning right along with my students." Her own questioning found its way into her curriculum as she taught her students to also question injustice that personally affected their community. The way in which her foundational thinking shifted within her teacher education program was revealed in how and what she ultimately decided to teach.

CASE 4: TRANSFORMATION

The cases of Grace and Cara demonstrate that when teacher candidates are able to change their thinking by learning about race and racism, these ideological shifts transfer into their curriculum. The final teacher case is Diana, who also exhibits how reframes in thinking can transform curriculum. For Diana, these transformations were immediate—as soon as she learned something new, she integrated it into her thinking and therefore her teaching.

Diana is a White woman of Portuguese and Italian heritage who is a mother of two boys. Slightly older than the other teachers featured here, she already had teaching experience working with adult learners. Like many White people of immigrant backgrounds, Diana initially struggled with identifying herself as White. "I would say if you'd asked me going into this program, 'What are you?' I don't think I would say White, because my whole life growing up, I wasn't necessarily a person of Color, but I didn't feel like . . . even when I look at the boxes, White isn't the one I gravitate toward."

However, unlike Dawn's resistance, the minute Diana started learning about race and racism in the program, her thinking about how she identified racially immediately shifted. "I've always struggled with this, but yes, I'm White, because I've experienced the privileges of Whiteness. . . . So for me, that was a big shift. It was saying, okay, I'm going to move away from that [denying Whiteness], because that isn't helpful, to, yes, I'm White. Yes, I experience privilege. What do I do from here?"

Unlike Dawn's anger in learning about White privilege, Diana quickly accepted the concept, changed the way she self-identified, and sought a corresponding action to go with this new knowledge. "If I acknowledge that there's White privilege, and then I'm acknowledging that I'm White, I'm also acknowledging that I'm a part of the problem, that I have some guilt to bear—not guilt, I don't know, responsibility to bear." In naming that she had a responsibility, she looked for ways to act responsibly.

Diane's action orientation also showed up in the way she started to think about the existing curriculum. When asked to reflect on the way she was taught social studies, she realized that, "It was easy for me to make connections to the history and social studies curricula as a child because they told the story of my ancestors." As she began to recognize that the curriculum would not reflect her students' history at the predominately Black elementary school where she was student teaching, she reflected, "It is in the consideration of these things that I find myself changing and developing as an educator. I have to say that from one of our earliest readings on *Deculturalization* and the Indigenous people, the ways I thought changed—and therefore the ways I teach are changing."[3] Here, Diana applied her new awareness of the prevalence of a Eurocentric curriculum to what it would mean for her practice. She was consistent in this process of integrating new information into a transformed action plan.

Like Cara, Diana did not interpret the justice-oriented content of the program as facts that needed memorization. Instead it became a new way of seeing the world—a transformed racial ideology. Diana began to think differently, act differently, and teach differently as a result of this new lens around race and racism. This new way of thinking was not relegated to coursework; rather it impacted her everywhere, even seemingly mundane interactions in her own home.

One evening, her sons wanted her to play superheroes with them and she agreed, as long as she could play with one of the girl superhero figurines. Sifting through the toys, it took a long time for her boys to find a girl superhero. When Diana then asked to play with a Black girl superhero, they realized there were none in their giant pile of toys. She revealed, "I was being a mom, tired, playing with her kids and just noticing something, and being like, 'Wow. What does that mean? What if my kids weren't White boys? What if I had a girl? What if I had a child of Color? Or a child who had a disability, right? What if any of those things? How would she feel? How would he feel?'" Diana's observation of the lack of diversity in her sons' toy pile set off a series of questions based on her new awareness of racial injustice. This aha moment in her living room led to the idea of the unit she wanted to teach her third graders, because, she thought, "If I'm this age and I'm just recognizing it, I think it'd be interesting to help students recognize that and what does that mean."

This set her on a journey of creating a unit similar to Grace's in which her students gathered data to determine who is represented in the superhero world. Her unit started with asking her students to name their favorite superheroes. After identifying their favorites in terms of race, gender, and able-bodiedness, the children then sorted and graphed the hundreds of superhero toys and playing cards that Diana brought from home. The results were devastating. The students' data analysis found that out of the 350 figures, 308 "looked like boys," 335 were White, and 349 were able-bodied.

Students felt that their findings were "not right and not fair!" The children were then asked to discuss who was not represented and to ask questions of power such as "Why do they all look alike?" and "Who do you think decides what superheroes look like?" This naming of power is what sets Diana's unit apart from Grace's similar approach. Whereas Grace stopped at the point where students noticed disproportionality, Diana taught them to go one step further and ask why and to name an oppressor.

It was through this line of questioning that Diana introduced students to an age-appropriate way of understanding the concept of *hegemony*, the idea that one group can consolidate power and dominance not just by force but also by manipulating mainstream ideology in such a way that makes the imbalance of power seem right, natural, and necessary.[4] She introduced them to a superhero villain she named the Mad Hater who hates identities other than his own. "The Mad Hater's superpower is that he can control people's minds and convince them that all superheroes have to look like him— White able-bodied men." Through the Mad Hater, Diana was able to teach how power and racism operate—in some ways exposing the Tools of Whiteness to her young students.

Remarkably, in an earlier reflection on an anti-racism training that was part of our program, Diana was struck by a quote shared by a facilitator of the workshop: "One of the first things I wrote in my notebook as we started the session was, 'The greatest trick the devil ever pulled was convincing the world he didn't exist.'" This idea kept nagging at her: "I kept coming back to that idea all day, especially from the lens of my Whiteness. . . . I found myself coming back to that idea that it takes a lot of strategic intentional work to get people to buy into the idea that the evil of racism doesn't exist." Although she didn't consciously make this association, there is a connection between Diana's revised thinking about race in the "devil" that she brought directly into her curriculum in the form of the Mad Hater. In the earlier case of Dawn, we saw her hegemonic, racist ideology creep into her curriculum in the same way that we see Diana's transformed thinking manifest in the lessons she teaches her children. In both cases, ideology is present in each curriculum, but the way in which they are willing to transform their thinking shifts their curriculum dramatically.

Once Diana introduced the Mad Hater, she led the students to question who the Mad Haters were in real life. Students identified comic book authors, movie directors, toy companies, and more. Just as Diana integrated new knowledge into action, she encouraged her students to do the same by asking them, "Okay, what would we say to superhero creators if we could to let them know this is making us mad and it's not fair?" She had the students brainstorm some ideas and pick ones they wanted to follow up with. She concluded, "I hope what they get from it is, don't just stop with the data. Do something with it." Her own habit of putting learning into action is evident in her curriculum.

Another new awareness Diana integrated into her ideology was the importance of community. "I think we are conditioned to be individualistic in our work and society. The Undoing Racism workshop helped me to recognize that fact as part of White culture conditioning." Diana shared her new perspective: "What I have learned through [my curriculum unit] is the benefit, the necessity, and my reliance on others to do the best work possible. Collaboration isn't cheating in this work—it's a powerful and necessary tool of resistance." Because Diana learned this valuable lesson about collectivity, it is not surprising that she wanted her students to learn it too. Her belief became integrated into her curriculum. A key part of her unit was to teach students to realize that it takes collective efforts to defeat racism by introducing the Social Justice League, which she described in the following way to her students:

> The Social Justice League is a superhero cohort whose mission it is to confront and disrupt social injustice, and its arch nemesis, the MAD HATER, a villain who uses mind control to convince the world that all superheroes should look like him. Students will be introduced to THE SEEKER to examine the concept of representation. Parallel to data collection and examination, students will investigate the ways that representation is tied to larger issues of racism, sexism, and privilege. ACCESS will introduce students to issues surrounding ableism. LIBERTY and THE GATEKEEPER will help students explore the ways in which laws and resources can help undergird or dismantle systems.

Just as was evident in her own transformed White-centered value of individualism versus collectivism, Diana taught her students the value of seeing the assets of all people, helping them recognize that it will take collective action to transform injustice.

SHIFTING THE DEFAULT SETTING TO ANTI-RACISM

Diana had a profound reflection in thinking about what it means to be White in America. She delineated levels of White awareness: "To sit there and think that racism doesn't exist is delusional. To acknowledge that racism exists but deny your complicity in it is self-serving. To acknowledge it exists but refuse to talk about it is a 'conspiracy of courtesy.' To acknowledge it exists, feel bad about it, but not think you can do anything about it is laziness." Diana realized that all of these ways of viewing racism in fact contribute to the perpetuation of racism. "What I found profound was this added layer to the idea that to sit there and to not commit yourself actively to an anti-racist lifestyle is, in fact, a default to racism. A default setting is the way a system is designed to function automatically without interference from users. The system relies on complacency to exist. Our country is literally on a default setting to racism."

As Diana contends, unless White people are actively committed to anti-racism, we will remain on the default setting of racism. This means that simply being a nice person is not enough; White people have to move from passivity to active anti-racism. Psychologist Beverly Daniel Tatum describes this move through the following analogy:

> I sometimes visualize the ongoing cycle of racism as a moving walkway at the airport. Active racist behavior is equivalent to walking fast on the conveyor belt . . . Passive racist behavior is equivalent to standing still on the walkway. No overt effort is being made, but

the conveyor belt moves the bystanders along to the same destina-
tion as those who are actively walking. Some of the bystanders
may feel the motion of the conveyor belt, see the active racists
ahead of them, and choose to turn around . . . But unless they are
walking actively in the opposite direction at a speed faster than
the conveyor belt—unless they are actively antiracist—they will
find themselves carried along with the others.[5]

Given that the vast majority of teachers are White and may not
have had the opportunity to examine their Whiteness, many of
them are moving passively on the conveyer belt. While only some
may be actively contributing to #CurriculumSoWhite, many are
doing nothing to interrupt it. In order to move in the opposite direction, or to turn off the default setting, teachers—and especially
White teachers—must examine their racial ideology and become
active anti-racists. In all four of the cases presented in this chapter,
there is a clear association between the way the teachers think about
race and what they hope their students will come to understand
through their curriculum. This demonstrates how important it is for
teacher education to explicitly address and transform racial ideology as a part of curriculum design. The chapters that follow provide
more insight into how to transform preservice teachers' ideological
understandings of race within teacher education in order to shift the
default setting off racism.

CHAPTER 3

REFRAMING UNDERSTANDINGS OF RACE WITHIN TEACHER EDUCATION

Not everything that is faced can be changed, but nothing can be changed until it is faced.

—JAMES BALDWIN

THE RACIAL HOSTILITY OF US SCHOOLS

In chapter 1, I looked at a disturbing pattern of how teachers' ideological beliefs about race find their way into their curriculum. Left out of this analysis are all the other ways these racist beliefs play out in the context of schooling, from discipline to environment to family relationships. Even as I write this chapter, two examples of teachers' racism went viral in the last few days. The first took place in Maine on October 9, 2019, where a White assistant principal called a nine-year-old biracial boy the N-word while disciplining him.[1] The second occurred in Pennsylvania two days later when a White teacher and a Black parent were involved in a fender bender in the parking lot during student drop-off.[2] The parent posted a video of the teacher's rant on Facebook in which she yelled at the father, "You're probably on welfare." The father responded that she was only saying that because he is young and Black, to which she responded, "That's right, [it's] because you're Black! Always looking to milk the system. And you see me, a White woman, so you think I got money. Go back to your welfare or your Section 8 house! Do you see the big truck I have? Look at the piece of shit you have." She went on to call him the N-word.

The epidemic of racism in schools is a boiling pot that spills over into every aspect of education. We have teachers in Idaho dressing up at Halloween as stereotypes of Mexicans behind a cutout of the border wall with a sign that says "Make America Great Again."[3] We have a teacher in Texas telling immigrant students, "Even though you are a citizen, Trump is working on a law where he can deport you, too, because of your mom's status."[4] There is a PTA in Brooklyn using photos of White performers in blackface for a fundraiser, and a teacher in Oregon berating a biracial nine-year-old, telling her she's lucky that "I'm not making you pick cotton or clean my house."[5] There is a teacher in Florida running a White supremacist podcast where she spouts theories about racial superiority in IQ's, while other teachers in California taunt Black students by posing for smiling pictures with an actual noose while making simulated neck-hanging gestures.[6] There are teachers who called the police to have a ten-year-old Black boy arrested for "assault" during a game of dodge-ball and to have a six-year-old Black girl arrested for an everyday six-year-old's tantrum.[7] The attack on children of Color in schools is incessant, terrorizing, and all-encompassing.

So while this book focuses predominately on curriculum, it is clear that teachers' racial beliefs create a hostile racial climate in all areas of education, transforming schools into sites of suffering for Black people and other people of Color.[8] Transforming teachers' racial ideology is therefore an essential strategy for not only addressing curricular Tools of Whiteness, but also for disrupting racism writ large. This chapter examines how the institution of teacher education can support this transformation. If we can support new teachers in understanding the full system of racism, we can encourage them to choose to dismantle it, rather than reproduce it, by setting aside Tools of Whiteness. There would be no need for a teacher to use such tools if their understanding of the world no longer aligned with the ideology of White supremacy.

RACIAL REFRAMES AND THE FOUR I'S OF OPPRESSION AND ADVANTAGE

Returning to the framework of the Four I's of Oppression and Advantage presented in the introduction, racism operates at four levels: ideological, institutional, interpersonal, and internalized. Teachers must recognize how this system operates at all four of these levels by learning particular racial literacies within each of the four domains. The Four I's framework is widely used in racial justice communities as an educational tool to understand how different types of racism support a larger structure. For example, a wonderful organization called the Center for Racial Justice in Education (CRJE) based out of New York and Dallas use it in their work with teachers and parents. A highlight of their workshop Talking about Race in Schools involves teachers role-playing different scenarios that could occur in classrooms and using the Four I's to identify how each scenario operates on multiple levels. In her book *Black Appetite. White Food*, education scholar Jamila Lyiscott outlines a compelling adaption of the Four I's framework called the Fugitive Literacies Framework. Lyiscott uses the Four I's to help educators recognize and categorize White privilege specifically, but then employs the Fugitive Literacies Framework to support them to author alternative ideologies, policies, behaviors, and thoughts that center racial inclusivity and equity.[9]

Rather than focus on the perpetuation of racism within the Four I's, I am using the framework here to identify how new thinking is required within each of these domains to develop critical racial consciousness. In this chapter, I use the Four I's framework to identify and categorize various racial reframes that White teachers must make in order to lay down Tools of Whiteness and work toward racial justice.

In his work on the troubling way the public views teachers, educational policy scholar Kevin Kumashiro relies on George Lakoff's concept of *frames* as ways of seeing the world. Similar to ideology, frames are invisible, unconscious ways of thinking that become normalized or considered common sense. The way we frame social phenomena such as race ends up shaping all Four I's, such as the policies we create, the interactions we engage in, and our own conceptions of self. In contrast, Lakoff explains, "Reframing is changing the way the public sees the world. It is changing what counts as common sense."[10] Kumashiro notes, "What we take to be 'common sense' is not something that just *is*; it is something that is developed and learned and perpetuated over time."[11] In my work with preservice teachers, my goal is to support them to recognize their common sense understandings within the Four I's so that they can reframe the way they conceptualize race.

In this chapter, I share a subset of findings from my research on preservice teachers and their conceptions of race.[12] This chapter focuses specifically on the racial reframes of White preservice teachers. These racial reframes align with the Four I's and demonstrate how these preservice teachers grappled with this reframing process. Their quotes represent snapshots in time and come from reflections they wrote about readings, workshops, and activities focused on race. Developing racial consciousness is an ongoing, challenging process, and these quotes demonstrate moments of struggle and disequilibrium as they moved from common sense thinking to a new awareness. I am not presenting these quotes as models of rightness—rather, they serve to demonstrate some of the authentic, messy, and emotional reframes that can be made when White people are exposed to a new way of understanding race.

IDEOLOGICAL RACIAL REFRAMES

The ideological domain of the Four I's framework consists of ideas of superiority and inferiority that are used to justify the other three domains. Ideological racism is often harder to identify because it has become so ingrained in the way our society is structured that these ideas about race rarely need to be said aloud. To reframe ideological racism, these unspoken, common-sense understandings need to be identified and deconstructed by learning the true history of how racism was constructed to justify settler colonialism and enslavement. Only by learning this history can people accurately identify how racism explains current patterns of inequality.

IDEOLOGICAL REFRAME: COMPREHENDING THAT
HISTORICAL RACISM SHAPED CURRENT INEQUALITY

The ideological reframe that seemed to have the biggest impact for the White preservice teachers I have worked with is understanding the role of history. As discussed in chapter 1, most White teachers were recipients of #CurriculumSoWhite when they were students, so it is little wonder that teachers' ideological understandings align with the "lies my teacher told me."[13] Without understanding the integral role that race played in the formation of the United States, there is really no way to comprehend the way racism stretches to every facet of life. In order to reframe ideological understandings of race, it is imperative that teachers receive substantial education about historical racism. As one preservice teacher contended: "I do not think that my own understanding of racism could have evolved without the clarity of [a] historical perspective."

Many White teachers have not been exposed to the history of race and racism. Once they get past denial, they often react with anger and resentment that they hadn't been taught it. Even in 2019, many of my students have only heard that Christopher Columbus "sailed the ocean blue." Simultaneously, cities across the United States are trying to change Columbus Day to Indigenous Peoples' Day and are being met with White rage along the way.[14] But without learning the historical record about the atrocities Columbus wrought and how he set the stage for settler colonialism, why would White people advocate for this change? Students who learned that Columbus was a hero could only be confused about what exactly needs to be fixed. Understanding history is the key element to reframing our understanding and joining others in advocating to set the record straight. You cannot set the record straight if you never learned that it is crooked.

After learning more about the history of racism through readings, activities, and workshops, most of my preservice teachers, of all races, have a hard time believing all the things they never learned. One student lamented, "So many things were omitted from my primary education, but I was also blatantly misled in my learning of the history of America." Some point to specific laws or policies that they hadn't known about such as "that the GI Bill segregated returning veterans by assigning jobs based on their function during the war, or that many Blacks were excluded from college because they could only attend historically Black colleges and universities, which were oversubscribed or located too far away." The cognitive dissonance of seeing history from a totally new perspective was enough to force most of my White students to make ideological reframes. As one preservice teacher illustrated: "It is dizzying to try to follow, especially when you first try to see the whole picture. I felt almost as if the curtain had been pulled back to show an entire other world which I had never seen before, even though it was right in front of me. Adjectives like *foolish, naive, stupid,* and *blind* poured through my thoughts." While this process can be painful and uncomfortable, it is an important step for making the huge cognitive reframes required to change White worldviews.

As my students worked through the deeply personal journey of realizing that their understanding of the world was based on a Eurocentric perspective, they began making connections to contemporary inequality. As one preservice teacher demonstrated, "It was intriguing to learn about laws that were put in place in the early colonization of America—laws that limited interactions between groups of people based on skin color, laws that discouraged and ultimately prohibited interracial marriage, and laws that initiated the idea of a racial hierarchy that continues to plague our society hundreds of years later." She went on to make connections to how this continues today: "It is still frustrating to think that these laws and events from several hundred years ago still plague our society on a daily basis." Connecting the dots between the historical foundations of racism and current inequality is key in being able to make the ideological reframes that are required for understanding systems of racism. Rather than believing in a level playing field in which individual effort is the lever for social change, the teachers began to realize that historical racist policy is responsible for intractable inequality.

IDEOLOGICAL REFRAME: PERCEIVING THAT RACE IS A SOCIAL CONSTRUCTION

Another important ideological racial reframe is recognizing that race is a social construction. Due to a lack of historical knowledge about race, many people do not know about how racial categories were created or the political nature of their creation.[15] Through participation in a two-day Undoing Racism workshop put on by the People's Institute for Survival and Beyond, a powerful multiracial organization out of New Orleans, my students learned to define race as "a specious classification of human beings created by Europeans (Whites) which assigns human worth and social status using 'White' as the model of humanity and the height of achievement for the purpose of establishing and maintaining power and privilege."[16] Through an overview of scientific racism, students were introduced to eighteenth-century scientist Carl Linnaeus's taxonomy of flora and fauna, *Systema Naturae*, in which he also classified four varieties of humans: *Europeanus* (white), *Americanus* (red), *Asiaticus* (yellow), and *Afer* or *Africanus* (black).[17] He placed *Europeanus* at the top of the superiority hierarchy, categorized as smart, inventive, and ruled by law. At the bottom of the hierarchy, *Homo Sapiens Afer* were described as crafty, careless, and ruled by caprice. The preservice teachers were also introduced to the Enlightenment-era anthropologist Johann Friedrich Blumenbach, who used the study of human skulls to justify a similar racial hierarchy that identified five human races: Caucasian, Malayan, Ethiopian, American, and Mongolian.

After learning that all humans are genetically 99.9 percent the same—and recognizing that what had been passing as "scientific" or "biological" categorization of race was a social construction used to justify European colonization and slavery—students reframed their understanding about how baseless the concept of race actually is. Learning that race is a socially constructed concept is a critical ideological reframe. As one preservice teacher expressed, "I was most on my growing edge when confronted by the idea that race is a social construct rather than an objective reality. I did not know that much of what we perceive as race is based on a classification system developed in the 1700s by White men who placed themselves at the top of a racial hierarchy." Understanding this history clears up many misconceptions about what race is. As one preservice teacher explained, "I have always thought of race as being based on skin color, hair color, and facial features but am becoming aware that identity is much more subtle and nuanced than that."

One potential pitfall some White people might make as they become aware that race is a social construction is to then dismiss the idea of racism. But as the popular saying goes, "Race is imaginary, but racism is real." It was through Natalia Ortiz of the Center for Racial Justice in Education that I first heard a helpful analogy she shared with my students during a Talking about Race in the Classroom workshop. She explained that money is also a social construction—simply a sheet of paper like any other. After she dared the students to rip up a dollar bill, she explained that because we have ascribed meaning to those pieces of paper and structured our society around them, the construction has very real consequences. This story helped my students realize that although race was made up, the consequences it has on our history and lived experiences are certainly real.

By expanding their understanding of how race is constructed and racism is maintained, White teachers can change their role in upholding systems of racism. Another preservice teacher reflected, "I never understood it [racism] as a system driven by ideology and institutions that I didn't create but could help perpetuate if complacent and neutral. But now that I am starting to [understand], I recognize that by its standards and society's, I am a White woman in America." Coming to see our place in the broader system of racism is a critical reframe required of White people who hope to take antiracist action. This reframe is necessary for breaking down the ideology of Whites as innocent and good that so many of the curricular Tools of Whiteness function to maintain. Using history to discredit this ideology, White teachers can make the reframes that will cause them to be less likely to teach and behave in ways that uphold this foundational ideology of Whiteness.

INTERNALIZED RACIAL REFRAMES

Shifts within the internalization domain focus on how teachers need to apply big picture ideological reframes to reshape their sense of selves. For White people, internalized racism is associated with how we have taken in and enacted messages of superiority and goodness. When explaining the differences in internalized racism between White people and people of Color, I often share a story that came up with a friend during grad school. We were both struggling with SPSS, a computer program for analyzing statistics; however, we placed the blame for our identical struggle in different places. My friend, who identifies as a Black Puerto Rican, was embarrassed because she felt too "dumb" to figure out the program. I on the other hand blamed the program for not being "intuitive" enough. I blamed the machine, she blamed herself.

While race seemingly had nothing to do with this situation, it demonstrates the way White people have been taught to externalize blame—in contrast to people of Color, who have been socialized to internalize shame and self-doubt. For her, not being able to figure out the program just added to the nagging doubt she had previously revealed to me about her identity as a scholar, making her wonder if she had been accepted into the program because of affirmative action. Being confronted with this computer program didn't trigger me into having imposter syndrome—or, in other words, doubting my place.[18] When we realized that we both were having such different responses to the same challenge, we were able to tease out the role that internalized racism had in it. This helped both of us to reframe the range of ways that we have reacted in various circumstances, recognizing the way internalized racial superiority and inferiority impacted so many aspects of the way we saw ourselves in the world. With this new awareness, I began to recognize aspects of my personality that I had thought had nothing to do with race as actually highly racialized. For example, I had thought of myself as naturally confident in my intelligence but came to realize this was in part a byproduct of being taught to externalize blame and internalize success as part of internalized racial superiority.

The creators of the online resource *Dismantling Racism Works Web Workbook* have developed a list of other ways that White people have internalized racial superiority. These include the following beliefs:

- My world view is the universal world view; our standards and norms are universal
- My achievements have to do with me, not with my membership in the white group
- I have a right to be comfortable and if I am not, then whoever is making me uncomfortable is to blame
- I can feel that I personally earned, through work and merit, any/all of my success
- Equating acts of unfairness experienced by white people with systemic racism experienced by People of Color
- I have many choices, as I should; everyone else has those same choices
- I am not responsible for what happened before, nor do I have to know anything about it; I have a right to be ignorant
- I assume race equity benefits only People of Color[19]

These beliefs serve as justifications for using curricular Tools of Whiteness; therefore, reframing these beliefs is a critical step in moving White teachers toward anti-racism. For White people to reframe within the internalized domain, we have to begin with a seemingly obvious but nevertheless challenging step—simply realizing that we have a race: we are White. This section examines some of the ways White people struggle with this step, including the benefits and biases that come with naming our racial identity.

INTERNALIZED REFRAME: OWNING A WHITE RACIAL IDENTITY

Recognizing Whiteness as a social construction begins to help White people see that we have also been racialized. As Dawn from chapter 2 finally acknowledged, "I never realized I had a race-type thing." Other preservice teachers were able to extend this recognition of White racial identity: "I had never really thought about myself being White and the implications of that classification. I realized that it makes me uncomfortable and guilty for taking this for granted. I am embarrassed that I have had my head in the sand." This racial reframe is uncomfortable, so it makes sense that we avoid having a White racial identity. Once it is named, we are forced to see how racism ultimately benefits us.

While this preservice teacher was able to get past her avoidance of owning that she was White, many other White people resist this, often by clinging to our national heritage or religion. I remember going to one of my first anti-racism trainings in 1998 called Beyond Diversity, facilitated by Glenn Singleton, an anti-racism thought leader and author of *Courageous Conversations About Race*. When he asked us to get into racial affinity groups, I went to the White table. However, a significant number of older Jewish participants refused to join us, demanding a racial affinity group for Jews, despite the fact that "Jewish" is not a race. As a Jewish woman, I remember feeling uncomfortable—I wanted to be respectful of my Jewish elders who had experienced anti-Semitism firsthand and whose generation was closer to the Holocaust. But to be honest, I was also tempted to go to their table because I could avoid the discomfort of having to go to the White table. However, something nagged at me that this too was privilege and a way to use my Jewish identity to avoid the responsibility that comes with identifying as White.

My students also identify with using cultural roots to disassociate with White identity. As one explained:

> Many White people would prefer to identify with their European cultural roots rather than just "White." Though I understand why people might want to distance themselves, I feel like it is extremely unrealistic and harmful for me to attempt to distance myself from my Whiteness. I have to own the "distasteful" parts of being a White person, be comfortable and ready to talk about being White, and live in awareness of my privilege.

Through owning their Whiteness, the preservice teachers reframed to see themselves as a part of, rather than separate from, a system of racism. Instead of relying on the way they had only racialized people of Color, they recognized that they, too, have a racial identity and started to notice the ways they resisted their own racialization.

I have found that more recent White immigrants, particularly those for whom English is their second language, struggle the most with this reframe. Unlike White Americans who have been here for generations, recent White immigrants might arrive here speaking another language and live together in close communities similar to Asians, Latinxs, or immigrants from the African diaspora. They have often faced discrimination because of their immigrant status. Therefore, these White immigrants identify more with the experiences of people of Color than with other White people and resist the racial identification.

I learned a way into this conversation through a story that trainer Bonnie Cushing, with the Undoing Racism workshop, shares with our preservice teachers. She talks about her Jewish family's assimilation into Whiteness and how many of the cultural practices of her family have diminished over time, starting with language and ending with food. As someone in the generation that follows her, I recognize this pattern with my own family. My immigrant grandparents strongly identified as Jewish: their temple was their community, and they spoke Yiddish, read Hebrew, and cooked Jewish foods. While my parents were active in temple in their childhood, as adults, they only attended temple for the High Holidays, fasted for Yom Kippur, lit Chanukah candles, and quickly forgot most Hebrew and Yiddish, except for a few colloquialisms. While I went to Hebrew school weekly until I was twelve, I was not Bat Mitzvahed and would go to temple only for my practicing cousins' life events like Bats Mitzvahs and weddings. While I have culturally Jewish idiosyncrasies, Bonnie's and my shared story explains all the cultural practices our families gave up to provide us with a full-access pass to the privileges of Whiteness. For my White immigrant students, recognizing that they are only a generation or two removed from "full-blown" Whiteness sets off a lot of challenging, but productive, self-reflection.

INTERNALIZED REFRAME: RECOGNIZING THE SYSTEMIC BENEFITS OF BEING WHITE

Understanding history, coupled with owning a White identity, supports teachers in recognizing how we are situated personally in the system of racism. One preservice teacher had a profound realization: "I don't know much about my family history, but I do know that I am related to several of the founding fathers of this country. It hurts to accept that the privileges that my family have were likely earned on the backs of slaves and that the disenfranchisement of people that I hope to work to help were likely caused in part by my own ancestors." This White aspiring teacher is applying her newly learned historical information to reframe her own original orientation of herself as a helper to one whose position of advantage was created on the backs of people of Color. This allowed her to move from positioning herself in a patronizing savior stance to recognizing the systemic forces that created the different levels on which she and her students are in terms of racial hierarchies.

Like this preservice teacher, understanding where our privilege came from helps us to reckon with ideas about ourselves, some of which may be valid and some of which could be associated with internalized racism. One of my preservice teachers grappled with the idea that race might have supported her outcomes: "In many ways I do feel as though I worked hard to get to where I am today. It was a blow to my own ego to consider that my race influenced my success, but I can now see that as a possibility." She was able to acknowledge that race played a role in her life outcome and continued, "It is scary to think that I might not be in the position that I am today if I were of a different race, and it is disheartening to know that others who have worked hard may never achieve to their full potential based on this same notion." Without this reframe, White teachers' work will drip with saviorism or charity. By recognizing that our Whiteness has set us up for success and set others up for marginalization, we are more apt to work to change an unjust system, rather than to "help" those who "just happen to be less fortunate." This reframe allows us to fight for justice by recognizing that injustice is a vertical fight against a system of oppression instead of holding a horizontal pity party for people of Color.

INTERNALIZED REFRAME: REALIZING THE BIASES THAT COME WITH BEING WHITE

One of the ways that the preservice teachers began to oppose racial hierarchies was to identify—even with the shame involved—their own internalized biases about people of Color. This is such an important step in moving away from curricular Tools of Whiteness because without checking our own internalized racist biases, we cannot recognize when our curriculum is reproducing them. By reframing our preconceptions and identifying how a system of racism instilled them in us, we can apply this reframe to all aspects of teaching, curriculum, interactions, family relationships, and so on. This makes anti-racism a stance instead of a box to check off. As one preservice teacher explained this process, she noted that she started to "question some of my underlying more deeply hidden prejudices: that poor people are that way because they are lazy, that people of Color don't succeed because they don't take advantage of the opportunities they have and then blame other people." She applied this thinking to her own outcomes: "Now I am realizing that the way society is set up does privilege me as a White woman and that I need to be aware of that and work to try and challenge systems that do perpetuate inequality." This critical internalized reframe is helping her to see how her judgments of others were based on false blaming (and lauding) of individuals instead of societal structures. By reframing their understanding of their racial identity and all that comes with owning it, the preservice teachers were able to move away from unquestioned internalized superiority. This allowed them to take responsibility, which prepared them to move toward anti-racism.

INSTITUTIONAL RACIAL REFRAMES

The institutional domain focuses on the ways that interlaced institutional structures (housing, healthcare, education, criminal justice, etc.) and their entwined policies and procedures were created by and reproduce advantages for White people while oppressing people of Color, especially BIPOC. Because White people benefit from upholding institutional racism, it is imperative that we understand our role in its reproduction and perpetuation.

Particularly in education, the relationship between institutional racism and the other domains cannot be underestimated. We have seen how the beliefs of White teachers manifest as institutional racism, influencing how teachers act as gatekeepers to resources, pipelines, and opportunities. A preservice teacher realized, "I learned that while I might not directly express racist sentiments, I am still in a position of power, just by default of being born a White woman, and thus am obligated to institute that power to oppose the currently existing racial hierarchies." In order to dismantle the systems that maintain racism, it is necessary to reframe how our positionality—not our intentions—provides us with power. In this section, the preservice teachers grapple with reframing their idea of teaching from a charitable act to instead reimagining their role as people who address institutional racism in order to move schooling toward justice.

INSTITUTIONAL REFRAME: REALIZING THAT
RACISM IS INSTITUTIONAL, NOT INDIVIDUAL

Many White people understand racism as personal ignorance and discrimination, rather than an institutionalized practice. By assigning the title of racist only to overtly racist individuals such as members of the KKK, White people can disassociate ourselves and our lives from the taint of racism. This disavowal maintains racial hierarchies, because if we don't think institutional racism exists, why would we be motivated to seek out systemic solutions? This way of thinking is directly implicated in how the examples of viral racist curriculum in chapter 1 were handled by admonishing the individual teacher, rather than addressing broader systems of racism. By scapegoating others, White people can maintain our position of innocence in the cycle of racism by claiming that we don't make racist comments or jokes and have never personally discriminated against anyone. This false framing serves to take the focus off the mechanisms of racism that are most damaging to people of Color and is therefore one of the most essential reframes in order to move toward anti-racism. One preservice teacher explained her own shift: "I had generally thought of racism as acts of hate toward groups of people different than one's own; I did not perceive racism in its relation to a system of power or privilege."

INSTITUTIONAL REFRAME: SHIFTING BLAME TO THE SYSTEM, NOT THE TARGETS OF RACISM

Educators are often charged with solving intractable social problems, such as equalizing educational outcomes for all students despite a lack of equitable economic and political power across different groups in society. If teachers cannot reframe, they will blame students and families and develop solutions that aim to "fix" people of Color. This process of blaming the victim locates the origins of social problems in those marginalized by oppression rather than in structural inequity and has four identifiable steps.[20] First, a social problem and the affected population are discerned, such as the so-called achievement gap that compares school achievement scores between Black and White students. Since Black students score lower in this achievement gap, they are framed as the problem to be fixed. Next, the values and behaviors of the targeted population are compared with those that are established as the "norm"—here, White students. Then, the source of the problem is identified as the difference between the affected group and the unaffected group—for example, Black culture, grit, intelligence, resilience, parental involvement—and finally, a treatment is created that tries to change the affected population, such as tutoring programs or parental involvement workshops.

This process allows teachers to rely on genetic and/or cultural explanations of achievement, placing blame on parents, "lazy" students, or culture while absolving educators or schools of any responsibility.[21] Rather than looking at achievement data in a vacuum, teachers committed to anti-racism must examine the social and economic conditions of different communities and reframe blame from the targets of racism to the system that perpetuates it.[22] Gloria Ladson-Billings reframed the achievement gap as the education debt and Asa Hilliard reframed it as the opportunity gap to refocus our attention on the differences in resources and opportunities among different groups of students.[23] However, the ideology on achievement that remains dominant reinforces deficit thinking that blames children of Color. Any solutions that come from this framing will target students of Color or their families as in need of being "fixed." The recent popularity of frameworks of grit and growth mindsets in schools are examples of such approaches, as they accuse Black children of being deficient in these areas and teach educators to "fix" something perceived to be missing in children rather than recognize the broader patterns of racism, trauma, and generational poverty that impact achievement.

By reframing from individuals to systems, teachers can move from deficit views that blame students and families to positioning themselves as people who understand how systemic barriers unfairly impact people of Color. One preservice teacher realized she was focused "primarily on the individual as a problem, as opposed to a systemic issue." As an example, she stated: "School has been in session for two weeks already and students are still struggling to bring supplies, and parents express they don't have money to purchase them." She started to reframe: "Instead of questioning why the New Jersey Department of Education or the Newark Public Schools do not include school supplies in their budget for each classroom, I blamed the students and families. Thus, my initial political view was focused on questioning the individual and not the systemic issues behind *why* this was happening." By shifting blame from those marginalized to the system, the preservice teachers refocused their direction for action. Rather than become frustrated with parents and frame them as "not caring about their children's education," White teachers can look to the systemic nature of school funding and make demands.

INSTITUTIONAL REFRAME: MOVING FROM CHARITY TO JUSTICE

As teachers reframe institutionally, they can start to ask different questions that can shift their target for change. As one preservice teacher suggested, "When we see an issue, we must figure out the root cause in order to make a permanent change. . . . We get so caught up in helping others that we forget to examine why others need the help in the first place. Why is there an achievement gap? Why is there overrepresentation of Black and Brown students in special education?" This preservice teacher went on to think about how this line of questioning shifted her thinking about her own role: "I wanted to work in an urban special education setting because I thought I would know how to teach these students and I want to help 'fix' the achievement gap. But now I find myself thinking about why certain people need to work harder than others, and why there even is an achievement gap or overrepresentation to begin with." By reframing her thinking about the role of institutional oppression, rather than targeting individual students, this White teacher shifted her self-image as a helper with all the answers to that of a person who questions broader societal structures.

This shift leads teachers to be able to work from an anti-racist perspective, rather than seeing their role as charitable or viewing themselves as a good White person for helping "those kids." When teachers work from a charitable perspective, they see themselves as pure-hearted for wanting to help students of Color. When teachers can reframe to start examining social issues, they can begin to question why some people are in need of help. Rather than make children feel more comfortable while experiencing oppression, teachers can start to change the conditions that leave certain people with less comfort.

This reframe from charity to justice plays a significant role in teachers laying down their curricular Tools of Whiteness for a number of reasons. First, they reframe themselves as good, charitable people to recognize how they have benefited from a system. They can no longer congratulate themselves and think that simply their presence in schools is enough, but instead, they must learn about systemic issues facing their students. It also shifts their curriculum from teaching that there is something wrong with people of Color to teaching about how to change systems. One preservice teacher depicted this shift by saying, "When educators understand the effects that institutional racism [has] had on these 'historically looted communities' and people of Color, they can work against these systems of injustices such as the school-to-prison pipeline, and educate children in a positive and culturally relevant way."[24] She warned of what happens without the reframe:

> On the flip side, educators who continue to perpetuate institutional racism hold the power to keep those who do not fit in with the ideals that society deem[s] desirable from doing well in school by labeling the child as having a behavior problem or referring the child for special education, or simply damaging the child's self-worth, which will likely, in some way, limit the child's ability to succeed. My goal moving forward as an educator is to ensure that I have no role in perpetuating these systems of oppression and instead work toward dismantling them.

INTERPERSONAL RACIAL REFRAMES

Many of the reframes within the previous three domains are cognitive shifts; they are about how we think about race writ large (ideological), how we understand power reproduction (institutional), and how we view ourselves (internalized). The interpersonal domain is where it all comes together because it is about how people engage across race. Through oppressive behaviors such as microaggressions, racist jokes, talking over, overlooking, and violence, White interpersonal racism is the behavioral manifestation of our beliefs in the other three I's. Because of the deep disequilibrium caused by reframing within the other domains, the preservice teachers became like deer in headlights trying to figure out how to engage responsibly with their new awareness, given the harm that White people have produced and continue to cause.

As these White preservice teachers prepared to teach in urban schools of Color, this disequilibrium raised a number of questions about their role. Themes from the data arose such as: "How can I, as a White teacher, be anti-racist in a racist system?" "How can I, as a White teacher, ever be accepted in a school community of Color?" "How can I, as a White teacher, teach from a culturally relevant perspective?" For example, one preservice teacher elucidated, "Previously I felt that, as a White person, I was in a position to address race. As a person who has not experienced racism, and instead has benefitted from it, how could I possibly be involved in a style of teaching that addresses and seeks to understand how my students have been on the opposite side of the racial system?" Just as I ask questions about my role as a White scholar working toward racial justice, asking oneself these challenging questions is part of the process of decentering the White tendency to think we can do whatever we want, wherever we want. Critical self-questioning is therefore a vital part of developing racial consciousness—as long as it does not become an excuse to retreat.

INTERPERSONAL REFRAME: BE COGNIZANT
OF IDENTITY WHEN TEACHING ABOUT RACE

One of the areas that caused the greatest apprehension for these White preservice teachers was teaching children of Color about race. For some of my more resistant students, this emerged from a fear that when students of Color learn about racism, they will hate White people writ large, but them specifically, potentially seeking revenge on them for historical actions. Other more reflective students worry about "getting it right." A preservice teacher grappled with it this way: "As a White person teaching children of Color, how do I decide what information is best for them? I can look at a curriculum and criticize it, but do I know any better?" The teachers were receiving the message that they needed to be culturally relevant teachers who create mirrors in the curriculum for their students of Color to learn about their own history, but as newly conscious White teachers, they had concerns. He continued, "I did not have the same experience growing up as these children have, and it goes without saying that good intentions do not mean much. I cannot help but feel uncomfortable at the thought of a White teacher thinking he knows best what children of Color should be learning. . . . This is a question I know I will struggle with for some time." This preservice teacher is in the midst of a productive struggle in which he is decentering his internalized sense of "White is right" and has started questioning his role as a White teacher. While it feels uncomfortable for him, this is a healthy place for us as White people to be in order to work to be accountable to people of Color.

Other preservice teachers worked through this struggle by becoming more comfortable with their own White racial identity. Diana, who taught the superhero unit in chapter 2 also named some of her initial discomfort: "I think I would have been too afraid to talk about race as a White woman in front of mostly Black students. I think I would've been too in my head about that and how to navigate it." Because Diana had reframed the other domains, she became capable of teaching her Black students about race: "Just being more comfortable with my racial identity so that I can be more comfortable. I want to see you, I want you to see me." Multiple domains of the Four I's are interplaying here—without owning her White racial identity (internalized), Diana would not have taught her Black students about how race operates (interpersonal) because, as she said, "I think I would have been uncomfortable with the data [of overrepresentation of White superheroes]; I don't know that I would have done it just out of my selfish discomfort level." Diana was able to implement a transformative, racial justice unit because she owned her White racial identity rather than deny it. She didn't just power through it or act like it didn't matter and like anyone can teach about race. Instead, she did the tough work of reframing within all the domains, which positioned her to be clear about the identity and power of both herself and her students. By laying all of this out on the table, she became comfortable and capable of teaching about race in ways that resist, rather than reproduce, racism.

INTERPERSONAL REFRAME: QUESTIONING WHITE CULTURAL NORMS IN SCHOOLS

Another area of disequilibrium was wondering how to interact with students in institutions the preservice teachers now recognize as racist. Through reframes in the institutional domain, the preservice teachers began to recognize how Whiteness informs what and how students of Color were being taught. As one preservice teacher illuminated her struggle: "Structures and systems have been set up with White cultural standards in mind. So much of being a 'highly effective' teacher has to do with classroom management, and as I am seeing firsthand, that really has to do with keeping students acting a very specific way." This preservice teacher began to question what that means for how she would balance what was expected of her and her new understandings of how race informs those expectations:

I am trying to reconcile that with internalized racial superiority. How do I, as a White teacher, walk into a classroom of mostly Black students, carrying with me the heavy baggage of racism, and then command control? And be evaluated on my ability to have the students remain quiet, seated, standing "heel to toe," ensure seamless transitions, while all the time urging them forward with promises of college, which will make them "successful."

She began to grasp that these values were not race-neutral: "All of which really means 'act like White people decided that successful people act.' And I am part of that system." This preservice teacher recognized the conflicting expectations. On the one hand, she was being charged with and evaluated for upholding disciplinary practices rooted in White cultural norms that mirror prison and military tactics such as silence, straight lines, and strict obedience. On the other, she was being taught in my program to share power and build humanizing, democratic relationships with students of Color. This is a true challenge for teachers dedicated to anti-racism who are working in institutions. Without the racial reframes mentioned throughout the chapter, however, she would have unquestioningly upheld these White cultural norms, been evaluated as highly effective, and felt good about the ways in which she "commanded control" over her Black students. By reframing her understandings within all four domains, she is able to racially analyze the way she understands her own Whiteness, how it informs her interactions with her students of Color, particularly those who are BIPOC, and ultimately the role that plays in reproducing or interrupting racism.

CONCLUSION

While I write here about how teacher education can better prepare anti-racist teachers, this chapter, surprisingly, is not about curriculum, pedagogy, instruction, or content. Rather, this chapter is about *thinking*. In order to work toward racial justice and to lay down curricular Tools of Whiteness, it is critical for those of us in teacher education to attend to what teachers think and believe about race. As demonstrated in chapters 1 and 2, White teachers who believe racist thoughts about people of Color teach racism. Because the beliefs lead to the teaching, it is imperative that we address the beliefs as part of any attempts to teach curriculum and instruction. By interrogating and reframing their beliefs, educators can design their curriculum and enact their instruction in ways that work toward racial justice.

Given all the knowledge and skills that teacher education already must impart while preparing new teachers, this presents a challenging dilemma. How can teacher education advance racial justice while also preparing teachers for all the other technical aspects of the craft? To answer this question, the next chapters explore the practices and structures of five teacher education programs in institutes of higher education with explicit racial justice missions. These programs provide insights for other institutes of higher education on how to prepare teachers who will not perpetuate #CurriculumSoWhite and instead will advance racial justice.

CHAPTER 4

DISRUPTING WHITENESS IN TEACHER EDUCATION

HOW CAN TEACHER EDUCATION DISRUPT WHITENESS?

As examples of racist curriculum continue to be exposed on social media, it is evident that schools of education cannot continue graduating teachers who are at best ill-equipped and at worst damaging for children of Color. Leaders of teacher education programs must take seriously the negative impact that Whiteness can have on all teachers' understanding of what and how they teach. As an institution, teacher education is one of the few places where pre- and in-service educators are required to be for substantive amounts of time. While there are many responsibilities that teacher educators must attend to, such as teaching disciplinary-specific content and methods courses, the pervasiveness of racism requires us to prioritize racial justice in preparing the next generation of teachers.

In the last chapter, it became clear that with focused energy, preservice teachers can, and do, make the racial reframes that are the prerequisites for moving toward anti-racist action. However, creating the space for preservice teachers to accomplish these racial reframes requires a massive overhaul of business as usual, which focuses mainly on the technical aspects of teaching. This chapter and the next one explore what it looks like to transform the institution of teacher education into a space that takes up this responsibility to racial justice. This chapter focuses on how teacher education can structurally arrange itself to respond to and disrupt Whiteness. The next chapter moves beyond just responding and instead shows how to shift to more humanizing relationships based on love and care.

Throughout these chapters, I discuss the variety of ways that Whiteness can show up in teacher education. By Whiteness, I am not referring to White people per se—I am talking about ways of wielding power and privilege that maintain White supremacy. Whiteness can be enacted by both White people and people of Color and can show up in many forms. For example, in teacher education, it can come from faculty who are opposed to addressing race, mentor teachers in the field who actively enact racism, or administrators who create institutional barriers to advancing racial justice. When Whiteness arises from students in class, it might be in the form of discrediting the existence of racism or asking why they have to keep talking about race. It might be a defensive denial of White people's culpability in a system of racism, or it might be a direct challenge to experiences of racism named by students of Color in class. Sometimes Whiteness shows up through people of Color's own internalized racism or through respectability politics in which students of Color express deficit stereotypes about the behavior of other people of Color—for example, middle-class Black students who characterize urban schools as "ghetto" or Latinx students who exhibit anti-Black beliefs.[1]

Disrupting Whiteness in teacher education requires an explicit, shared commitment among all stakeholders to center race and address racism. The established structure of higher education can make this challenging for various reasons. Teacher education programs are housed in colleges of education that offer a range of degrees and certifications. Teacher credential programs are often considered the cash cows of colleges of education because they bring in large numbers of tuition-paying students seeking a variety of credentials required by states in order to pursue teaching careers. Colleges of education are made up of faculty and administrators with a wide range of expertise and disciplines, as well as a wide range of racial ideologies. This context makes it difficult to achieve the kind of shared anti-racist agenda needed to advance racial justice. In fact, such programs and departments often, directly or indirectly, perpetuate racism and create hostile learning environments for students and faculty who are BIPOC.[2]

When they do attempt to implement change, justice-oriented administrators and faculty often struggle to transform these monoliths toward spaces of racial justice because of the lack of a shared racial ideology, pressures of external accreditation, and the need to recruit justice-minded faculty and students, among a host of other challenges. As a way to advance racial justice in teacher education, justice-oriented administrators and faculty at some universities have instead found ways to create smaller, mission-driven programs that I refer to as *racial justice programs* (RJPs). Through external grants, pilot programs, smaller initiatives, or changes in leadership, RJPs tend to operate slightly autonomously from their more traditional teacher education programs. Instead of ignoring race, relegating it to one course, treating it as an afterthought, or giving it one week on a syllabus, these RJPs are spaces that advance racial justice by centering race, disrupting Whiteness, reframing preservice teachers' understandings of race, and preparing and sustaining candidates for anti-racist action.

To learn more about the structure and pedagogies of such

programs, I interviewed eight teacher educators/administrators who work in five different RJPs. Because I codirect an RJP myself, I am including my own insights where relevant. The interviewees gave permission to use their real names. All of the interviewees, except Bill Kennedy and myself, are people of Color. While much of the actual work of these programs is based on supporting individual teacher transformation, these programs demonstrate the kind of institutional and programmatic design required to accomplish those transformations.

PROGRAM	POSITION	NAME
Center X at University of California, Los Angeles (UCLA)	Executive Director	Annamarie Francois
Center X at University of California, Los Angeles (UCLA)	Professor	Tyrone Howard
Newark Teacher Project (NTP) at Montclair State University	Codirector and Assistant Professor	Tanya Maloney
Newark Teacher Program (NTP) at Montclair State University	Codirector and Associate Professor	Bree Picower
Teacher Education Program (TEP) at Harvard Graduate School of Education	Director	Christina "V" Villarreal
Urban Education and Social Justice Program (UESJ) at University of San Francisco	Department Chair and Associate Professor	Patrick "Cam" Camangian
Urban Education and Social Justice Program (UESJ) at University of San Francisco	Assistant Professor	Farima Pour-Khorshid
Urban Teacher Education Program (UTEP) at the University of Chicago	Instructor	Kay Fujiyoshi
Urban Teacher Education Program (UTEP) at the University of Chicago	Former Codirector	Bill Kennedy

MOVE RACE FROM THE MARGIN TO THE CENTER

Unlike traditional programs, RJPs have moved race from the margins to the center in every conceivable way. Bill Kennedy delineated the evolution of the UTEP program he formerly directed at the University of Chicago as it transitioned to become an RJP over the course of five years. "The program evolved from just a course. In its earliest inception, there was recognition that this work [racial justice] was necessary, but it was treated very lightly so as not to offend." Kennedy explained that addressing race "was done outside of the core coursework and kind of seen as an addition."

As Kennedy and the program's other leader, Kay Fujiyoshi, took on more responsibility of the program, they transitioned this racial justice work into the core of their program. They expanded the course in terms of meeting time and frequency and included a community engagement field component, ultimately meeting for a full day each week. This also allowed them to shift the content of the original program. "We took an existing core sequence that was called 'academic strand' where a lot of educational theory readings were taught and said, 'Why is the race stuff sitting outside of this? Actually, race needs to be what we're reading centrally in the program.' So we took those two courses and put them together and expanded the time each week that it could be meeting." Because of their central focus on racial justice, they shifted the structure of their program: "I think a program has to see that work [racial justice] as the center and then go out, as opposed to an add-on." By moving racial justice to the center of the newly expanded course, UTEP was able to prioritize this content, making it clear that it was a hallmark of the program and not an add-on that happened outside of dedicated meeting time.

BE EXPLICIT ABOUT RACE FROM THE BEGINNING

One way that RJPs address Tools of Whiteness is by being explicit from the beginning, from marketing to admissions, that race will be centered. Students need to be aware that racial justice is a mission of the program and that they should expect to discuss it in all spaces, because racism lives everywhere. In fact, as this section will show, the RJPs are explicit about naming that racial justice is a priority from the beginning, during admissions, in their courses, with their faculty—everywhere. For example, when I first attempted to start my own RJP, an administrator told me that I should not put a small line at the bottom of the marketing flier that read "Students of Color are encouraged to apply" because I might lose potential White students.

As the program, and my authority over it, has expanded, our NTP flyer now has a photo of five alumni of Color and states: "NTP seminars support all areas of teacher development with a special focus on social and racial justice. The small cohort provides support and community and has access to many special events and high-quality anti-racist professional development." This explicitness is one way that RJPs disrupt Whiteness, as Whiteness relies on being masked, invisible, and unspoken.

BE EXPLICIT ABOUT RACE IN ADMISSIONS

All the RJPs in this study fronted racial justice as a core value of their mission. In the program I codirect with Tanya Maloney, we have added questions to our program admissions interview protocol specifically for White candidates so that they have all the information they need to choose to join us. For example, in interviewing a White woman for the Newark Teacher Project, I explained: "This program is made up of predominately students of Color. If accepted, you may be one of the only White people in the program. We will spend a lot of time talking about race, and we will not center your feelings in this process. Describe how this makes you feel and how you will handle it." I also described scenarios that have actually happened that require a certain amount of comfort with racially explicit, cross-racial interactions: "You are eating lunch with your mentor and her colleagues who are all Black. They start talking about how White people are ruining Harlem. How will you engage in this conversation?"

By being explicit about race from the onset, the interview becomes a two-way street. For the candidate, it simulates the nature of the program clearly enough that they can make an informed decision on whether they want such an experience, mitigating the surprise and resistance from students who aren't expecting, and don't want, to address race. In terms of admissions data, it allows us to see if the candidate has a self-reflective disposition or if they respond defensively. As chapters 2 and 3 demonstrate, White candidates don't need to come in knowing everything there is to know about race; rather, they must have the capacity for self-examination to make racial reframes.

BE EXPLICIT ABOUT RACE BY FORESHADOWING THE EXPERIENCE OF CENTERING RACE

Knowing the terrain of race-centered discussions, RJP faculty foreshadow what the experience will be like for their students, surfacing common tensions and feelings that are likely to come up. Annamarie Francois, the executive director of UCLA's Center X, tells her candidates:

No matter what your racial background is, no matter what your economic background, [addressing racism] is going to be difficult. What we want to do is make sure that we give you the knowledge and the tools and the opportunities to engage in civil discourse

around these really challenging issues. And as my colleague
Dr. Howard reminds us, we are asking that when you get uncomfortable that you sit in that discomfort. That you engage, rather
than resist.

She helps her students understand that one of the reasons they need
to feel that discomfort is "because that's the feeling that most of our
poor Black and Brown students feel in schools, every single day."
Because of their experience in centering race, the faculty know the
very specific types of resistance that are likely to emerge and work to
name them upfront rather than wait for them to appear. The faculty
understand that resistance is part of the process, but they know that
digging into and understanding the discomfort will make their students better, more critical, and more empathetic educators.

With all of their experience centering race, the faculty know
that, despite the foreshadowing, there will still be times when White
students will express anger and resistance in ways that cause harm
to the community. Christina "V" Villarreal, new director of the
Teacher Education Program at Harvard Graduate School of Education and former director of the MAT Program in History/Social
Studies at Brown University, prepares her students to navigate and
move through this experience, teaching them how to work through
challenging cross-racial dialogue. From the beginning, Villarreal
foreshadows what might happen in such discussions. She explains
that in one of the first conversations she has up front, she tells them:

> You better be ready. You're going to fuck up. You are going to make
> mistakes; you better accept it. You're going to inflict harm; the
> question is, one, when you make those mistakes, are you going
> to be prepared to hear it and accept responsibility for the impact

of your actions; and two, are you committed to then repairing or helping to heal the harm that you created or inflicted on the other side?

By foreshadowing the process and how to overcome challenges, RJPs support their candidates to move past the common enactments of Whiteness when learning about race, developing them into teachers with the capacity to advance racial justice.

BE EXPLICIT ABOUT RACE FROM DAY ONE IN COURSEWORK

In addition to admissions and foreshadowing, another way that race is explicit from the beginning is by fronting concepts of race in initial coursework. RJPs don't wait to bring race into the curriculum; they start it on day one. As Farima Pour-Khorshid, an assistant professor in the UESJ Program at University of San Francisco, declared, "I think it's problematic if we don't make [our focus on race] clear and understood day one at orientation." For most of the programs, initial coursework provided the opportunity to lay a foundational racial justice framework upon which all other learning would build. As Maloney, who codirects the Newark Teacher Project with me at Montclair State University, described of our family of RJP programs, "The initial summer class the students took in the program was about race, class, and identity. It was a class that essentially was intended to develop the students' racial identity, their understanding of their internalized race and racism, and their understanding of socio-political issues." This theme of fronting race in initial coursework was echoed throughout the other RJP faculty interviewed.

While most of the programs start with a broad framework such as the Four I's,[3] the UTEP program is unique in forefronting the realities of institutional racism in Chicago through an intensive field component. Fujiyoshi explains: "The foundation sequence begins with neoliberalism, class issues, and housing—and race is obviously central to that. There's some introductory work that I would call intro to critical race theory. Critical pedagogy sits in the philosophy course that is in the first year." Whether through initial orientations or embedded directly into first-semester coursework, all of these programs center race from the get-go.

DISRUPT WHITENESS IN CLASSES

More often than not, Whiteness will show up when educating White students about racism. Despite all the groundwork to prepare them that this is going to happen, and explanations of what it will feel like and how they will act, it is simply part of the process. I recognize this phenomenon from my experiences teaching about race, but also from my own responses to learning about race as a White woman. Over my lifetime of examining race and my own Whiteness, my reactions have shifted and transformed from those early feelings of shame and defensiveness that my students feel to a constant questioning of myself, my role, and my reactions through the lens of privilege and superiority.

This examination itself, however, does not preclude me from still enacting Whiteness. For example, reading, studying, and teaching Robin DiAngelo's seminal book *White Fragility* doesn't mean I don't still *feel* White fragility when called out/in on how my own Whiteness is manifesting itself. The benefit of doing the work of anti-racism is that I can at least recognize and name the feeling of fragility and remind myself to step back, take a breath, and reframe. Learning about and disrupting Whiteness is a lifelong process. Similarly, White students, despite their progressive nature or their good intentions, are going to enact their Whiteness when learning about race.

Unlike many traditional teacher education programs, however, RJPs anticipate that Whiteness will emerge and are prepared with strategies to address and disrupt it. As stated by Patrick "Cam" Camangian, an associate professor in the UESJ program at University of San Francisco, "It's inevitable that you would always have a White woman, one who might be speaking for others [resisting the content]. This is a common thing that's happened across about six different courses that I taught." As Fujiyoshi explains, RJPs don't avoid those conversations—they use them. "A lot of things surface during the quarter, especially in these conversations around identity, and so we don't shy away from it, we delve into the wreckage, as Bill Ayers talks about, and we sit in it. We see what's around, and then we plot forward." This section examines some of that wreckage and what it looks like to plot forward toward racial justice.

BE EXPLICIT WHEN ADDRESSING STUDENT RESISTANCE

Despite all the strategies to prepare students for the explicit emphasis on racial justice throughout the RJPs, this focus in classes still sometimes comes as a surprise to some preservice teachers, particularly White ones. When this happens, faculty continue to be explicit about the importance of the racial justice focus. Tyrone Howard, professor and director of the Black Male Institute at UCLA, described a White student who, despite the explicit racial justice mission of the program, enrolled only because UCLA was her dream school. He remembered how she was initially very quiet when topics of inclusion, race, and colonialism came up in the first course sessions. The student went to his office hours and expressed her concern to him: "I didn't know this class would be so much about race, or that the program would be so much about race." He explained to her: "Part of what we think is important in this work is that context matters, and the context for Los Angeles is that it is one of the most racially diverse places on the planet, and we need you to understand that history of race and racism, racial justice, and racial exclusion."

As expected, she responded with the "I just want to be a good teacher" script he had heard many times before. Howard continued to be explicit about the racial justice mission of the program: "I get that. But we think that part of being a good teacher is understanding the racial context. You cannot disentangle the two. So we had that initial conversation." By helping students unpack why this explicit mission on race is needed, the RJPs disrupt the resistant Whiteness aimed at derailing their racial justice focus.

WHEN WHITENESS SHOWS UP, MAKE IT A PART OF THE CURRICULUM

Regardless of how Whiteness manifests in classes, it must be disrupted. Because of the lack of training or preparation to center race in teacher education, many faculty outside these programs don't know how to respond. Tyrone Howard explains, "It's the stuff that's unscripted that puts most of us into these real awkward positions. Someone says something highly inappropriate, and everyone looks at the instructor. She or he doesn't know what to say or how to respond, so they don't respond. And then there's silence." Sometimes, the instructor does not know what to do, and other times, they don't want to move away from their syllabus or what they had planned for the day. Howard continued, "I have colleagues who are very much linear, type A, and feel like 'I've got to get to these five things today and I'm not going to allow the course to go off target into something that's tied to race or any other matter because then I can't get to my five things.'"

In contrast, RJP faculty believe the conversations that emerge from disrupting Whiteness *are* the curriculum, not a detour from it. Howard explains that if he doesn't get through the five things, "I'm completely okay with that because I think [dealing with issues of race] is much, much more critical to their development as teach-ers." Similarly, Kennedy also values what happens when addressing Whiteness in class: "When there's some kind of microaggression in the class and people are like, whoa, and everything sort of breaks down, then that becomes the fabric from which you can re-ally have those conversations . . . as opposed to talking abstractly about some sort of theory or reading about it from a nonfiction perspective."

Pour-Khorshid described what happened when Whiteness mani-fested itself, this time from a student of Color who stated a racist idea in class: "We stopped and we had to really unpack and we just wrestled with these ideas, and a lot of the students ended up going back to the text. . . . So I think in the end it was a really rich discus-sion." The faculty recognize that these conversations are critical and model for students how to hold this space in their own classrooms. But addressing these teachable moments also presents a challenge when forced into the confine of courses that have prescribed con-tent. Pour-Khorshid adds, "I will say it does take hella time and when you are expected to deliver a certain amount of content, packed into certain weeks . . . but I know they'll never forget that moment." In a traditional program, this concern around covering the official cur-riculum takes precedent over the detour, whereas in an RJP, address-ing racial justice is also considered curriculum, so space is allowed for it.

ALLOW RACIAL CONFLICT TO ERUPT

When race is front and center in coursework, it is not uncommon for racial tension between students of Color and White students to flare. While these tensions may simmer in classes that don't address race, in RJPs they are addressed head-on. RJP faculty address these racial conflicts by first allowing them to happen, then unpacking what is behind them, and finally creating the space to heal. Howard gave an example that represents a typical way in which these situations emerge. He remembered a class where racial tensions flared. "In particular, several students [of Color] said, 'One of the things that White people need to do' or something like that. I think that was a trigger for her [the White student] that they mentioned 'White people' as opposed to, say, 'Whiteness.' I think she took exception to that." In response, the White student tried to separate herself from the White people they were talking about. She started listing all the ways she had served students of Color in the past. This only exacerbated the frustration of the students of Color, who knew this avoidance strategy of Whiteness all too well.

Howard continued: "The student who was Latinx was trying to convey to her that even though she may have done some work with communities of Color, by no stretch of the imagination did that give her reprieve from being one of the 'White people.' So it got kind of heated and I had to intervene. I let it go for a while, and then I felt like, okay, maybe it needs some cooling off." As a skilled racial justice practitioner, Howard knew when to let the tension build, how to release it, and, most importantly, how to turn it into a teachable moment. He explains how he handles these situations. "We will not try to just acknowledge [Whiteness] and then move on real quickly. There's a conversation. Part of what I try to generate is a multitude of perspectives to understand why people feel the way that they feel. It gets emotional. It gets heated. It can be very tense. I think those conversations are good. I think they're important."

Howard clarifies how these situations ultimately serve to support the White students as future anti-racist educators: "Because I think they as teachers need to understand, they need to feel the emotion and the pain and the anger that some of our students of

Color feel when these bouts of Whiteness manifest themselves." By feeling their peers' anger, the White students more deeply witness the depth and pain of racism, which in turn better prepares them to understand their future students' struggles.

In Camangian's class, a similar eruption happened. Because his program actively recruits activist students of Color, they are unapologetic about letting White students know when their Whiteness is showing. Camangian recalled a class where a student of Color responded to a White student's comment dismissing racism because she claimed that as a woman, she was also oppressed. The student of Color announced, "That's this White shit. You just did all this privilege. You don't even fucking know it. You have lots to learn—fuck your gender studies."

Camangian says, "White women try to find that point of solidarity in these arguments saying things like, 'You're not the only one who's oppressed,' and they'll like go to these places and say, 'I grew up poor,' and all this stuff." Like Howard, Camangian sees the benefit of letting the tensions manifest, but he also understands the costs and his responsibility in rebuilding the community. "It is hard to heal from or to recover from. You have to have that plan. And then, I'll do a circle." Here Camangian is referring to a restorative circle used as part of a practice of restorative justice for the purpose of holding students accountable, repairing harm, and moving forward as a community.[4] As part of this process, he asks the students to reflect: "What was that like for you? What's your point of view? How do you feel about moving forward? Everybody gets their say and it'll feel better, but it's still hard to recover from."

Camangian understands the way that White students avoid race by clinging to other marginalized identities. He uses the racial conflict in class as a strategy for disrupting this by creating space for the voices of students of Color to speak out. By strategically allowing racial conflict, the faculty in RJPs allow the racial tensions that emerge in cross-racial education to serve as another text for disrupting Whiteness.

In reflection, Camangian explained that for the White students, "I think it was one of the first times where White privilege, White supremacy, or White positionality was named in real time for them by critical students of Color who have a scathing analysis. They say it the way they feel it." The labor of the students of Color also taught White students how to move toward anti-racism by stepping out of complacency and sharing the work of disrupting Whiteness. For some of the White students who he describes as more on the fence, "they would sit there and they would process it. They will try to understand and observe how that impacted the more resistant White folks, and they were called upon by the folks of Color to help share the responsibility—emotional labor, if you will—to work with the White folks who were pushing back."

Camangian reported that several of the White students were able to pick up this charge and engaged in calling-in conversations with resistant White students. As a result, they also developed meaningful cross-racial relationships. *Calling in* is a strategy of having accountability conversations that help people understand and shift how they may be reinforcing problematic systems of power in their behaviors. Calling in emerged as a response to *call-out* or *cancel culture*, in which offending individuals are shamed publicly and excluded from a continued presence in a community. While the push from their peers in these call-in conversations was integral to some of the White teachers positioning themselves as co-conspirators, it leaves the question of how RJPs can accomplish this without the emotional labor of students of Color.

ENSURE THERE IS NOWHERE FOR WHITENESS TO HIDE

Returning to how RJPs center race, this section focuses on how the programs ensure that students' Whiteness is interrupted. Often, students might say the right thing in class but then enact racist practices in their student teaching placement, or vice versa. To ensure that a student's growth toward racial justice isn't performative but rather is a true ideological reframing, RJPs are determined to ensure that all program team members share a commitment to racial justice so there is nowhere for Whiteness to hide. As Tanya Maloney described, "Any one moment could be a moment that needs to be disrupted, and so no one person can be there for everything. There are more places where Whiteness gets disrupted that might not exist in a program where everyone isn't making such a concerted effort toward thinking about these issues." By ensuring that all program team members share this same focus, Maloney explained how students are surrounded by people with a shared understanding about race. "The same people that are going in to do observations are thinking about race, the people that are designing and teaching the coursework are thinking about race. The mentor teachers in the classroom are developing their understandings of race. There is nowhere to hide." In this way, students must truly transform their understandings and behaviors because it is unlikely that they can keep up an anti-racist charade within all areas of the program.

As an example of this nowhere to hide concept, I recall a day in our RJP when mentor teachers were on campus with faculty for professional development, and a mentor teacher received a text of a photo taken by a paraprofessional in her classroom. The photo was of a racially problematic and confusing math word problem being taught by one of our White preservice teachers. This preservice teacher was already on our radar because of some offhanded, questionable statements she had made to a group of Black mentor teachers. The quality of her assignments had also prompted us to create an improvement plan with her that served as a contract for areas in which she needed to show progress in order to remain in the program.

Because of our shared commitment to racial justice, and because the program had developed our close-knit relationships, the mentor teacher immediately showed the photo to the RJP team. The director, field supervisor, mentor, and I quickly developed a plan of action to address the situation. All of us shared a commitment to fostering the learning and teaching of racial justice and understood the severity of the situation. As the White person on the team, I made the first call to the student to learn more about her intention with the word problem. When her response came from a place of defensiveness and anger, rather than humility and openness, it became clear that further actions were needed.

As we typically do, we scheduled what Jennifer Robinson, our executive director of the Center of Pedagogy, refers to as a 360 support meeting in which all the team members who engage with the student came together to develop a plan and to then meet with her. Our first attempts were to support her continued development and to better understand what her intentions were behind the word problem in question. However, her response to our request to meet was to enumerate her complaints about her mentor, the paraprofessional, professors, and the director of the program. Outside of myself, all of these individuals are women of Color. As we continued to ask her to reflect on this pattern of displacement rather than reflection, her engagement devolved into defensive, rambling emails filled with expletives. These behaviors are now associated with a popular culture identity referred to as "Karen," which has become shorthand for White women who weaponize their resentment toward and entitlement over people of Color.[5] Her fragile response to being asked to reflect on a single word problem made it clear to us that she could not be held accountable for her own behavior, to women of Color, or to the children she would be responsible for teaching; therefore, she could not continue in our program. Had the program team not had a shared commitment to racial justice, students like this one could easily slip through the cracks and end up in the classroom harming children who are BIPOC through curricular Tools of Whiteness. But because of the 360 support, there was no place for her Whiteness to hide.

BE STRATEGIC ABOUT RACIAL IDENTITY

An important aspect of 360 support is that it is not race evasive. It is important to consider the race of the student and faculty involved and to be strategic about who should provide the intervention. Often when issues arise with students of Color, it is important to ensure that a program team member of Color is the lead support so that the student can better focus on the message and not the messenger. For White students, it is often important that a White faculty member take the lead because White students experiencing White fragility can act out against faculty of Color. This strategic and overt consideration about faculty racial identity is talked about more openly in RJPs than in traditional programs, where faculty racial identity either goes unnamed or is used in tokenizing ways.

In this example from Christina Villarreal, she shared how her team members had an explicit discussion about their racial identities in strategizing how to engage a resistant White student. In this situation, Villarreal sat down with the field supervisor, a White woman who Villarreal describes as "deeply committed to racial justice." The supervisor told Villarreal about how the student was presenting her defiance. Villarreal and the supervisor agreed that the student's behavior was unacceptable, but the field supervisor wasn't sure how hard she should push the student. Villarreal told her, "'To be honest, as a White woman to another White woman, I expect you to go harder than I can, as a woman of Color.' She was like, 'Great, I just wanted a green light. So I'm going to push her on her racial analysis and how she's been teaching.'" Villarreal stressed the importance of this kind of racially strategic collaboration, explaining that the supervisor "has also struggled and oftentimes feels in a silo, so when we were able to join forces and collaborate, I think we felt, it isn't always just on us."

Villarreal also pointed out the challenge of getting White people to engage the way this field supervisor did. "I've noticed that oftentimes the mentors and the advisors of Color are more direct in coming to me. I feel like when it's like White mentors and White advisors, I tend to have to take that step toward 'Hey how's it going with that student,' whereas the women of Color have come to me."

Unlike these White mentors, it is deeply important that White program team members doing this work understand their responsibility to do the heavy lifting and pushing when it comes to disrupting Whiteness. Kennedy recognizes his role as a White person in his program this way: "There was just a sense, especially if it was a White candidate, of 'Bill, you need to go talk to him or you need to go talk to her,' because some of that work has to be shared across faculty racially, so that folks of Color are not doing that work all the time." This strategic use of racial identity is yet another way that RJPs provide 360 support in ways that affirm and push all students in their development toward racial justice.

HAVE AN EXIT STRATEGY

Despite the best efforts in offering 360 support, sometimes it becomes clear that a candidate is not a fit for the classroom. A responsibility RJPs take seriously is gatekeeping who will end up standing in front of young people—especially in front of students of Color. Ultimately, it is up to us to make the call as to whether our preservice teachers have the dispositions and skills to build caring relationships and provide culturally sustaining instruction or if they are going to be the ones who end up on Facebook enacting #CurriculumSoWhite.

Part of the challenge with this role is that assessments within traditional teacher education programs mainly measure coursework and student teaching, not dispositions such as anti-racism. A preservice teacher who may enact their Whiteness in the classroom can slip through the cracks by being a straight-A student who behaves with outward respect to authority when needed and meets all the minimum requirements. Within these contexts, teacher educators in typical programs often have little ground to stand upon for wanting to dismiss candidates such as these who may have made an inappropriate comment once or twice but who otherwise checked all the programmatic and academic boxes.

CREATE STRUCTURES TO COUNSEL STUDENTS OUT

To ensure they are graduating teachers aligned with their missions, RJPs have developed strategies to document and systematize exit strategies for students who they feel may ultimately do harm to young people. One way they accomplish this is to apply a racial justice lens when using mainstream, race-neutral standards of assessing teaching, such as teacher expectations, classroom management, and lesson instruction. In her work in multiple RJPs, Villarreal has used this strategy when it is clear her candidates have not made progress in their racial literacy and she needs to counsel them. She explains that even when students have technically done the graduate level work, it is "part of my life job [to] figure out how to use these structures to our advantage to do this work through an anti-racist lens."

In order to get past the challenge of exiting students who have "done the work," she looks at state standards through an anti-racist lens, seeing where Whiteness shows up in ways that she can gather as evidence that candidates are not adequately serving all students. "[Racism] shows up as instruction and execution of a lesson, which is tied to high expectations and how they're interacting in the classroom. That's where I can actually gather data on things like problematic interactions between White teachers and young Black male students. That is probably what I see the most. And that's something I can have actual data to utilize."

As RJPs gather data, their first strategy is to provide the 360 support described earlier to try to redress the problem. Unfortunately, despite this support, it sometimes becomes clear that the student is unwilling to grow. Through their experiences, RJPs are able to identify particular indicators of resistance. One such indicator is when students are unwilling to reflect or take on the stance of a learner. Villarreal explains that in her lesson observation debriefs with students, she will "start with asking questions, like, 'What happened here?' The red flag and the hard stop is when they are blaming everything on the child and not taking any responsibility."

The UTEP program addressed this common phenomenon by having explicit expectations and a code of conduct specifically about student dispositions. This allows Kay Fujiyoshi to ask critical questions that provide evidence as to whether the student has potential to advance in their racial literacy. She asks, "'Are you coming from a place of learning, or are you coming from a place of opposition? Are you taking into consideration what we're saying to you or are you an externalizer?' So we're actually monitoring this in our candidate assessment document . . . things like humility, that has to do with how you're receiving feedback." This document is used throughout the candidates' entire time in the program to track growth or stagnation. As Fujiyoshi concludes, "For some folks, it means getting coached out of the program. . . . It's kind of a given that you shouldn't be racist, it's a given that you shouldn't just 'act White' wherever you go. These are the things that we're going to be focusing on because that should have been nipped in the bud first year." Through experience, RJPs understand that ideological transformation is mitigated by certain dispositions and that without evidence of them, some students cannot become the kinds of racial justice educators the RJPs aim to graduate.

Racial justice leadership is a key support for exiting such students. While traditional programs feel pressure to graduate every student for their statistics, RJP leaders understand the goals of the program and trust those closest to the students. Maloney described the hierarchy of support that we have experienced at Montclair State. She says, "Our deans, department chairs, and the director of the Center of Pedagogy that houses our RJP have supported our program in various ways. When we do have a challenge with a student, [our leadership] immediately respond and want to talk about how they can provide support or how can they support us in exiting the student. They believe us to know this preservice teacher is inflicting harm and trust that that's the case. That sort of trust is all the way up the pipeline, if you will, the chain of command." This trust allows the RJP to make the tough decision of exiting a student. This decision is often heartbreaking because for many of our candidates, we are in the position of ending their lifelong dream. But we must remember that, ultimately, it is not our candidates we are accountable to as teacher educators.

BE ACCOUNTABLE TO CHILDREN OF COLOR

I remember receiving some marketing materials about fifteen years ago for Bank Street College promoting their teacher education program. I can't find the original image, but what I recall is a picture of a young teacher being interviewed in front of a panel. What intrigued me about the image was that the panel was not made up of stereotypical principals and administrators but rather by elementary-age children of Color. I carry this visual in my mind to remind myself that as a teacher educator, it might appear that I am accountable to my teacher candidates, but it is to the children they will ultimately serve that my accountability lies. It is my responsibility to the children to ensure their teacher is worthy of them.

The teacher educators in this chapter take a similar view when they have to make the tough decision to exit candidates from their programs. As Villarreal expressed passionately, thinking of her former students from when she was a teacher and high school administrator in California, "I don't think that everybody belongs or is worthy to be in front of our babies, and I'm always thinking about my babies in Oakland. I'm not accountable to this [institution]; I feel accountable to the young people in classrooms."

Annamarie Francois takes a similar stance with her unwillingness to allow schoolchildren of Color to be guinea pigs for harm-causing teachers. "Ultimately, we're unafraid of counseling people out. . . . It's the ones that you think, this candidate is going to further traumatize our young people . . . and if they go into our schools with this kind of deficit mindset, it's not fair to our young people and it's not fair to the candidate either." She recounted a story in which she exited a student and his father, a "muckety-muck" lawyer, called her, cursing. She unapologetically told him, "'Your responsibility is to your child, and my responsibility is to every child that he potentially would be teaching for his entire career. And I cannot allow that to happen.' That dad was cursing at me like you would not believe. And I was just like, 'You can curse me all you want to, but he's still not gonna finish this. Our kids deserve nothing less.'" This unapologetic allegiance to children of Color is embedded in the mission, philosophy, and structures of the RJPs.

This chapter explored what this commitment to disrupting Whiteness throughout the program looks like in practice. The final chapter continues this focus on RJPs, but it examines who needs to be at the table to realize such a vision and commitment to racial justice. By focusing on finding and developing the right students and program teams, RJPs not only disrupt Whiteness but also model the kinds of loving and humanizing relationships that move us from disruption to liberation.

CHAPTER 5

HUMANIZING RACIAL JUSTICE IN TEACHER EDUCATION

Do you want sweet poison or do you want bitter medicine?
Bitter medicine sucks going down. But sweet poison is
just going to kill you in the end. So which one would
you rather have?

—KAY FUJIYOSHI, TEACHER EDUCATOR

While the last chapter ended with strategies for disrupting Whiteness by counseling certain people out of the field, this chapter focuses on recruiting mission-driven people into it. From students and faculty to mentors, field supervisors, and community-based organizations, nothing is more vital to advancing racial justice in teacher education than ensuring the right people are around the table. This chapter explores how the Racial Justice Programs (RJPs) work to develop like-minded program teams with shared vision and how they recruit students with the most capacity to teach toward anti-racism.

Gathering all the right people is like assembling essential ingredients, but it isn't enough—you still have to make the recipe. Racial justice in teacher education is humanizing work that requires critical relationships and individuals willing to hold the emotions that arise out of the work of deep reflection. Author and education scholar

Bettina Love proclaims that "we want to do more than survive." While the introduction and previous four chapters of this book focused on surviving Whiteness, the kinds of relationships developed in the RJPs begin to move teacher education past surviving and invite the possibility of becoming spaces for thriving.

DEVELOP A PROGRAM TEAM WITH A SHARED MISSION

RJPs are particular about who needs to be at the table when advancing racial justice in teacher education. They tend to take a team approach and seek to have a say in all the people who interact with their preservice teachers. While that includes faculty and administrators, such as those interviewed for this book, it also includes advisors, field supervisors, adjuncts, classroom mentor teachers, and school leaders. The RJPs work to ensure a shared political analysis amongst the team. Bill Kennedy explained, "There was a recognition early on that [the cohort] could not be taught by a singular person, I think in part to combat the idea that this should be on the back of one person. Also because the person who was doing it originally recognized quickly that he was not prepared to do it by himself as a White person." The RJPs thought deeply about who should be around the table, in terms of racial identity but also disposition and skills, and therefore dedicated time and resources to hiring, professional development, leadership, and ongoing reflection. This team building was a key component because it ensured that candidates received the kind of 360 support needed to prepare them to advance racial justice in their future classrooms.

POSITION LEADERSHIP TO HIRE QUALIFIED
PROGRAM TEAM MEMBERS COMMITTED TO RACIAL JUSTICE

Finding the specific and sophisticated skill set for such a wide range of roles is a challenge. It is made easier when leadership at the top understand the racial justice goals of the programs and seek qualified people. As the leadership recognizes who needs to be at the table, systems and hiring can shift to ensure that other critical team members, like mentor teachers, are brought into the program as well. For example, when it was time to hire a new director for the Newark Montclair Urban Teacher Residency Program that housed the RJP programs at my institution, myself and other like-minded colleagues volunteered to be on the hiring committee. This way we could try to ensure that the new director would be (a) a person of Color, (b) a person with demonstrated experience in Newark, and (c) someone with a social justice mindset. Because we also have supportive racial justice leadership from our dean and the director of the Center of Pedagogy, we were able to hire someone who fit the criteria, Kimberly R. Santos. She in turn set off a chain of hires, as well as transitions out, that literally and figuratively changed the face of our field mentors and induction coaches to become almost exclusively women of Color, and predominately Black women.

Each RJP emphasizes how important it is for them to have control over hiring people with the specific identities, experiences, skills, and perspectives for preparing anti racist teachers. Recruiting BIPOC is a consistent goal. Christina Villarreal has come to recognize the inherent power in hiring as a tool for advancing racial justice in the programs she has led. "As a director, I have agency around hiring. So who did I hire? If you look at my team of field advisors, it's nearly all women of Color, with a couple of White women, all of whom demonstrated an explicit commitment to racial justice during the interview process." Villarreal clarified that this is a shift from the identity of past advisors. "It goes back to the same criteria around admissions: What am I looking for in an application?" While hiring people of Color was a priority, the applicant's experience and perspective on justice mattered, which moved the hiring beyond tokenism. "I changed the requirements of the advisor position to say 'has to have explicit experience with and commitment to asset-driven and justice-oriented curriculum and pedagogy.' I think that actually weeded out a lot of people who would have applied for the same position in past years."

For one of the interviewees, gaining hiring privileges was a battle they chose to fight when first taking on leadership in the program. They said, "I want to have fucking hiring privileges. I want to increase the number of critically conscious teachers of Color who are teaching our teachers. I want more queer teachers, and I want to increase the number of teachers who could help all of our teachers grow." This RJP had attempted to address this dilemma by hiring alumni of Color, but they recognized that while the alumni had the right racial identity, teaching experience, and political analysis, they didn't yet have the experience to navigate White resistance from students. "They didn't have the experience to take the emotional labor off of those experiencing the brunt of these biases. So despite being 'of Color,' they were still placating even to the comfort level of those who were invested in the existing social system."

This reveals how specific the skill set is to advance racial justice in teacher education. RJPs have to consider identity, teaching experience, racial/political consciousness, content area expertise, *and* the ability to navigate and disrupt Whiteness. For the last criterion, the interviewee described a goal of teacher educators who can "help support multiply marginalized students in those spaces to feel heard, recognized, and seen as experts on their own reality, while at the same time not altogether silencing White students." They had to jump through a lot of hoops and engage in several political navigations in order to gain the right to make those desired hires. They finished: "Just to be clear, I have the final say on hiring. Which was my way of saying, fuck the way you did it, I'm handling shit now."

Annamarie Francois explained that the qualities Center X looks for when staffing their teacher education program are aligned with their racial justice mission and how that mirrors what they also look for in students. "We're essentially looking for the same thing, but at a higher level. So what we oftentimes say in the Center is that one of our guiding principles is that we need to mirror the diverse, critical thought–carrying, social justice–oriented communities that we seek to create in schools. So that means the Center has to reflect that." The teacher education courses at Center X are taught by UCLA faculty who have advanced degrees and are considered experts in their field, but that is not enough for them to be automatically selected to teach in the RJP. Francois elucidates: "They play this border-crossing role; they understand the intersection of research and practice, but they also understand what it means to work in low-performing urban schools, because they attended and/or taught in urban public schools, so there's not a private school teacher mindset on the team. . . . We get to decide who teaches, so we cherry-pick educators whose beliefs and values align with ours and whose research can help inform the way we carry out teacher education." RJPs understand the importance that every team player has in reframing the ideology of preservice teachers and therefore dedicate the time and resources to ensuring that hires at every level have both the requisite skills as well as a shared dedication to and experience in working toward racial justice.

In addition to hiring, assistance from leadership involves navigating external entities such as funding and accreditation. Tanya Maloney explained the support from our leadership: "Because they trust that we are doing work that is purposeful and that is good for our students, they support us by continuing to apply for grants to support our work."

On top of finding funding, racial justice leadership involves sheltering RJPs from external pressures that could easily derail them.

One such pressure is accreditation. Institutions of higher education are bound to both national and state accreditation requirements to demonstrate both legal compliance and adherence to the curricular and program standards required of educator preparation programs. All too often, these standards privilege more technical dimensions of teaching over racial justice components. In her leadership role over Center X, Francois has made a political commitment to defending her program against the ways in which traditional accreditation demands are out of touch with a racial justice framework. In describing her program review experiences, she reflected, "If you don't understand the language of critical race theory, if you're not committed to educational justice in the way we think about justice, it'd be hard for you as a reviewer to see how all of those technical aspects of teaching are embedded in our justice-oriented program. The technical takes second seat to why we do things the way we do—cultural relevancy, cultural sustainability. It was really, really hard to explain that." Fortunately, she believes that thanks to increased dialogue between the accreditation body and teacher educators, the evaluations are starting to become more aligned toward the asset-based approach of RJPs.

DEVELOP A RACIAL JUSTICE COMMITMENT ACROSS ROLES

Oftentimes, RJPs struggle to find classroom teachers to serve as mentors who are not only successful teachers with strong content, pedagogical, and relationship skills, but who also advance a racial justice mindset. Efforts to find mentors who are people of Color doesn't necessarily mean that they have advanced racial justice knowledge. Additionally, typically there is not alignment between the racial justice goals of the programs and the daily demands of the realities of classrooms. Therefore, preservice teachers find themselves growing in terms of their racial analysis from coursework but may find themselves in conflict with their classroom mentors, or they are blocked from implementing the kind of racial justice curriculum assigned within the RJP.

The systems in place for recruiting mentors in many traditional teacher education programs look more for typical criterion for highly qualified classrooms, so RJPs need to do additional work in finding and vetting mentors to ensure an ideological and pedagogical fit. At Center X, since field advisors were selected to lead cohorts because of their commitment to racial justice, they are entrusted to find these multidimensional classroom mentors. Francois explained, "Our faculty advisors are responsible for finding the placement, vetting the placement, talking with the principals about the beliefs and values of the program, making sure it's a good fit—and not just around the technical dimensions of teaching, but around the social and political dimensions as well."

Despite these efforts, finding people with all the right criteria is a challenge, so one strategy is to provide professional development (PD) around racial justice for people who fit the bill in terms of other qualifications and identity markers. Traditional professional development for educators is often imposed by administration and delivered by outside curricular vendors or consultants based on discrete skills. While mentor teachers may be required to attend PD to learn certain curricular programs, they often do not receive support in how to mentor—and even more rare are opportunities to develop consciousness around racial justice.

In contrast to traditional PD, critical professional development (CPD) is a type of development that "frames teachers as politically-aware individuals who have a stake in teaching and transforming society. In both pedagogy and content, CPD develops teachers' critical consciousness by focusing their efforts towards liberatory teaching."[1] It is with this model of CPD that the Newark Teacher Project supports mentor teachers in developing their political understandings of racial justice. Maloney explained:

> Our mentor teachers spend the most time with our students, so it's important that their professional development is really focused on preparing anti-racist teachers as well. We do that by inviting our mentors to engage with our students in the very same curriculum that we have our students engage in. So for example, this summer, as a part of the initial mentor institute . . . they were learning about the Four I's framework and thinking about how to connect that to understanding education.

Because of the challenge of filling roles with people who fit in terms of identity, skills, and shared commitment to racial justice, oftentimes RJPs take on the additional work of providing critical professional development to all team members.

COLLECTIVELY ENGAGE IN THE INTERNAL WORK OF RACIAL JUSTICE

Given the challenges of hiring for, developing, and engaging in racial justice work, there is a need for continual growth and learning. Farima Pour-Khorshid recognized that as teacher educators, "none of us have arrived to a point where we don't need to engage in this deep, reflective, and emotional work." She wondered, "What does the preparation for teacher education look like and how are we creating space for teacher educators to do their own work too?" RJPs must carve out the time, space, and resources for team members to do the tough work of continuing to advance our own personal and professional racial justice knowledge, engage in critical self-reflection, and interrogate and heal our deep-seated racial ideology.

Pour-Khorshid calls on RJPs to create "more intentional space of doing this kind of internal work as well. Not just sharing how we're doing it in our courses, but literally personally doing it." While she recognizes that not everyone wants to do that work, she believes that "it would be a powerful way to model a more holistic approach to advancing racial justice." Pour-Khorshid challenges us to do this internal work "in a way that is nonhierarchical, in a way that is grounded in cultural humility, in a way that's really about humanizing ourselves as professors and humanizing our students and really seeing it as a reciprocal process, as opposed to teaching theory to our students in transactional ways."

UCLA has taken on some of this collective internal work. Tyrone Howard described how the faculty has engaged in conversations about race and diversity over the past few years. He reflected that "those have been fruitful, in my opinion, because those are spaces where we as a faculty come together to talk about our own stuff, if you will. Because it's one thing to say, 'You need to be more racially just and inclusive,' but there's something different to sit in a room as part of a two- or three-day retreat." By personally unpacking their own "stuff," the RJPs are engaging in the very same work they ask of their students, therefore gaining more insight and empathy into the emotional aspect of this endeavor.

This internal work is not without its challenges, given that Whiteness lives not just with students, but within faculty as well. Francois recounts, "I don't want to make it sound as though racial justice is easy and we have all the answers. It's not, and we don't. It's really hard because we bring our own identities, our own histories, into the work, but I think that we have a willingness to go there with one another. And we have enough patience, just enough patience, that when it gets hard, we still sit at the table." This willingness to go there ensures that Whiteness is interrupted not only with students but also with faculty.

Francois remembers, "There are times when we have some

White faculty members who get very emotional when we're tackling issues of racial justice and when we use words like 'White fragility,' like 'White supremacy.' When we are speaking our truth and speaking from who we are, it doesn't sound academic, right—it sounds like Annamarie, curly-haired Brown girl that grew up in South LA. That's the way I'm engaging in those conversations. With all my lived experiences as a Brown girl from South LA." Francois's willingness to be vulnerable supports others around the table to reframe their own racial ideology:

> But we still have White teacher [educators] that cry, and at the same time we have teacher [educators] of Color who were raised in middle-class, upper-middle-class families who also have challenges with some of these conversations. The point is, we all have challenges with these conversations because we are likely to come into it with our own stuff. But you got to be willing and to hold the expectation that in this teacher education program, we're going there, and if you're not willing to go there, then this is not the right fit for you. We have had teacher educators who have left.

As typically happens, it is the emotional generosity of people of Color such as Francois who take up the labor to have challenging conversations that pushes the work forward. Their unwavering commitment to racial justice in the classroom and the conference room sustains and refines the work of the RJPs.

RECRUIT AND ADMIT CRITICAL PRESERVICE TEACHERS

Just as the RJPs are intentional about building program teams with shared missions, they are equally intentional about admitting critically conscious students into their programs. Previously, I wrote about admissions being a place to be explicit with students about the racial justice mission of the program. I write more about admissions here to demonstrate the way these programs selectively screen to ensure they have students who can become strong teachers for students of Color. Because students typically complete their teacher education programs in one to two years, RJPs must attend to the justice-minded dispositions potential candidates exhibit at admissions. We have a finite amount of time to transform preservice teachers' ideology. If we are to take up the mission of advancing racial justice, we have to be honest about how far we can actually move those who come in with explicitly racist understandings coupled with resistance to alternative views. If we can admit that it would take more than a year to prepare some students to become the kind of teacher students of Color deserve, then we need to apply that political clarity within the admissions process and provide some level of control over who will become teachers.[2]

In moving toward racial justice in teacher education, all of the RJPs are resolute in their commitment to recruiting students of Color. In fact, a program I initially interviewed for this chapter was an urban teacher education program at SUNY Cortland called Cortland's Urban Recruitment of Educators (CURE) that is exclusively for teachers of Color.[3] Similarly, Francois stated, "We specifically recruit teachers of Color. That's our target audience. Most of our students have reported that they come to UCLA because they know someone who's gone through the program, and they know they're going to be seen and they know that we're going to surface—not just surface, but we're going to grapple with—White supremacy, racial injustice, identity, and positionality."

While the RJPs prioritize candidates of Color, they also accept White students. However, for all their applicants, the programs put into place screening processes because they want to specifically recruit critically conscious students who are looking for an anti-racist experience. Camangian recounted, "We've historically been the program that brought in the students of Color that brought critical consciousness, the White allies, and those on the fence who we felt had potential as agents of social transformation." Pour-Khorshid, who teaches in the same program, added, "We're selective. One: prioritizing students of Color from marginalized backgrounds. Two: students who are committed to wanting to do that work [racial justice]. They may not even be hella critically conscious, but if they have a desire and a commitment to do that work, then that matters." To help tease out which students want to do the work of anti-racism, there are certain questions their program asks. Pour-Khorshid provides insights on these: "I think it's more around why they even want to come into the profession. Questions like that are really important and will set other students apart and helps us to figure out who would be the right fit for that kind of experience."

There is a saying that traditional teacher education programs, as the university cash cows, are pressured into accepting anyone with a bank account and a pulse to keep enrollment high and money coming in. In contrast, Francois explains what they are looking for in candidates during the admissions process: "So when we recruit . . . we evaluate them on their experience in urban settings, their experience in schools, their commitment to social justice, and then their ability to analyze and respond to, in writing and verbally, a piece of academic text around some kind of an issue that requires courageous and critical conversation."

Fujiyoshi demonstrates how their similar admissions process serves to screen people in as well as out. She recounted an interview where they asked candidates how they felt about having conversations about race. One of the candidates answered, "I'm really looking forward to having dirty conversations about race." She pressed back: "Dirty is a really interesting adjective to use. Why did you do that?

Why was that your word choice?" His inability to articulate why he characterized race as "dirty" or to engage further about the topic gave them enough hesitation not to accept him into the program. She said, "Those are the things that are on our radar from admissions where we're just like, I don't know if we can work with you. There's a certain level of what we can and cannot work with, and I think our admissions process does a good job of giving us at least a starting point."

The admissions screening makes it clear that for some candidates, there isn't enough time to get them where they need to be within the confines of the programs. To be introduced to diversity and racism, see it through an asset rather than "dirty" lens, reframe all Four I's, *and* learn to teach is too much of a lift within the short time they are in teacher education. By applying this kind of clarity during the admissions process, these programs are able to focus their energy on candidates who are further along in their development of becoming racially just educators.[4] As Francois explains, "While we have them, we want to make sure that we shift their mindsets as far as we can toward being critical social justice educators in the limited time that we have. At least they go into schools with some beginning tools. We may not have gotten them [all the way there], but at very least, they will do no harm."

BUILD RELATIONSHIPS THAT HOLD EMOTIONS

Once the program team and student cohorts are in place, the real magic of the RJPs begins. With so many people committed to the same vision of racial justice, RJPs are able to create the context for powerful and humanizing relationships where people are truly seen, trust is developed, and the vulnerable work of deepening racial consciousness can blossom. Relationships, trust, and care are hallmarks of the RJPs and set the groundwork for the racial justice work. As

Patrick Camangian asserts, "Students don't care how much their teachers know until they know how much their teachers care." Similarly, Francois stresses, "Teaching is 90 percent about relationships. And relationships are dependent upon my being able to see you, to understand you, and to value you, and then help you get to where you want to go."

In alignment, Villarreal avowed that: "Teaching is only 20 percent content, but 80 percent relationships." Teaching, she explained, "starts with being able to meet your students where they are," which is why she works to develop relationships with her preservice candidates. "I can't train you until I know you and you can't work with kids until you know yourself." Her teaching philosophy is grounded in her ethnic studies background that posits, "No history, no self; know history, know self." As a result, she creates multiple opportunities to build personal relationships with each student and to develop community across students. Through these relationships, students are able to dig deeply into their own personal and cultural histories to prepare for similar work with children. She builds these relationships by creating a rich array of social activities in which the community gets to know each other as whole people, rather than just in their professional roles as students and professor. These activities include inviting her cohorts to dream up and wear group Halloween costumes, hosting baking parties at her home, traveling on wine tasting tours, and going out for karaoke parties. These activities create opportunities for the students to deeply connect and for her to get to know their personalities, hopes, and fears. By investing in these relationships, Villarreal builds trust with her candidates and, as will be demonstrated, trust sets the context for the vulnerability to push toward racial justice.

These caring, critical, and humanizing relationships fostered between faculty and their candidates are not feel-good popularity contests or attempts to be liked. Rather, they build the trust necessary for the challenging emotional component of advancing racial justice. Education leadership scholar Rosa Rivera-McCutchen uses the framework of *radical care* to describe such practices that focus on challenging broader inequality while cultivating authentic relationships.[5] The radical care in the student-teacher relationships within the RJPs is authentic, but it is also intentional because it is within these relationships that the deeply vulnerable work of dismantling Whiteness happens.

Bill Kennedy unpacks the balance: "There's a caring aspect, an empathizing aspect, that happens. But there's also then a chance to push." He describes this radical care as "messy." "We have boxes of tissues just piled up in our office because we expect that. And I think you have to have the kind of disposition to want that." Kennedy explains that the faculty indeed want and set the stage for these relationships because they are purposeful in creating the space for growth. "I'm not treating this like a psychologist or anything, but for my own work around this [examining race], I feel that's an aha moment when I know something's happening—that's when there's some learning going on." These humanizing relationships, characterized by trust, facilitate the capacity for both faculty and students to do the tough, emotional work that is part of interrupting a lifetime of socialization into Whiteness.

TEASE APART AUTHENTIC EMOTIONS FROM STRATEGIES OF WHITENESS

Supporting candidates to do the kinds of racial reframing evident in chapter 3 is challenging and emotional. Particularly for White students, resistance and Tools of Whiteness are also part of this process of examining race, so it is important for faculty to be able to recognize the difference between authentic emotional growth and White resistance strategies. By building humanizing relationships with students, faculty are able to know students well enough to be able to tease out which is emerging.

In 2019, activist and lecturer Rachel Cargle was featured in the *Washington Post* with an article titled "I Refuse to Listen to White Women Cry."[6] In it, she described her responses to her audiences of mainly White women: "When women have come up to me crying, I say, 'Let me know when you feel a little better, then maybe we can talk . . . If you have feelings about it, take it to your therapist, because this is not the space.'" As hinted at in the Cargle article, the term *White tears* has become popular in anti-racist circles in the last several years and refers to the way White people, particularly women, take up space and derail interracial dialogue by exhibiting emotional distress when topics of Whiteness are raised. White tears are a strategic tool of Whiteness to pull the empathy in the room toward their user, positioning White women as the ones who need comfort and attention in challenging race conversations rather than the people of Color who are the actual targets of racism.

To move students forward in reframing race, RJPs complicate the notion of White tears and recognize when crying is derailing versus when it is authentic. As Villarreal explained, "I think there's different variations of tears. There's obviously the tears of shame. There's tears of guilt. But I also see tears of growth, and those are powerful because they're accompanied by statements like 'I never thought about it that way before.' That, to me, is the opposite of a red flag; it's a green flag." Pour-Khorshid also teased apart the way some of her White students respond to race content, explaining, "Being connected to feelings is different from taking up space. How you do the work to unpack those feelings matters, your willingness to engage in that deep critical self-reflection and labor to learn and heal makes all the difference." These professors' ability to tease apart the different types of tears and emotions their students exhibit goes back to the deep, personal, radical care they put into each of their students, because only that allows them to properly assess where their students' emotional responses are coming from.

Fujiyoshi explains the complicated emotions that White students experience during conversations about race. "Those are difficult for a lot of White folks. There's a lot of guilt or shame or really feeling scared to mess up. And I think those are good emotions because they show you that you care enough, that you are worried about this, that you're thinking about it, it's on your radar. But it's tiring. Everybody cries." Creating the relationships that allow for this flow of emotions is part of the work of dismantling Whiteness, and it takes years of experience, empathy, and emotional labor to be able to decipher the source of the exhibited emotion.

In contrast to the productive emotions described above, Fujiyoshi is able to identify when White students are instead using emotions as a strategy of resistance. "That's another thing that I wrestle with—just feeling like the White folks need some more validation, they are looking for me to say 'great job.' But when the push comes and they're being challenged in some way, then it becomes, 'It's you, Dr. Kay, who's making me feel like this!' and then it becomes this externalization thing." Fujiyoshi's skill and experience allow her to distinguish when the emotions come from internal reflection versus external resistance. Because of the trust she builds, she can continue to push them forward, despite their resistance. She profoundly responds to her students by asking them, "Do you want sweet poison or do you want bitter medicine? Bitter medicine sucks going down. But sweet poison is just going to kill you in the end. So which one would you rather have?" Through this choice, Fujiyoshi makes it clear that while these relationships are loving, they are also places where unapologetically tough work is going to happen.

The trust built within these relationships prepares students to understand that when they are called in about something they have said, it is meant as a way for them to grow and learn, rather than as an affront to their character. This work of unlearning racism is not a walk in the park. Pour-Khorshid warns her students, "Don't be offended if I gently and lovingly let you know what you just said was foul, and we're going to unpack that together. It's always a learning opportunity." Students understand that what they do or say will be held up to them like a mirror—but because of the gentle and loving relationship, the bitter medicine is more likely to be seen as an opportunity for growth and less likely to be read as a personal attack.

RECOGNIZE THE EMOTIONAL TOLL

While the RJP team members recognize the vital necessity of this humanizing work, holding these emotions takes a toll on them, particularly on faculty of Color, who are navigating the unexamined racism of their White students and supporting the internalized racial trauma of their students of Color. For faculty of Color, navigating the balance of protecting themselves from the racism of their White students while also simultaneously using the program to push students' anti-racist development places them in their own space of vulnerability.

In the UTEP program, Fujiyoshi meets with every student individually in meetings called one-on-ones to check in and help them work through their growth. Fujiyoshi describes the toll of these meetings: "The one-on-ones are exhausting. There are a lot of tears, it's a lot of time. For me, it's a lot of headspace and a lot of worrying." Traditional teacher education methods classes on math or reading instruction are less likely to take on this emotional side. One interviewee described a methods instructor in their department who was "an older White guy, nice as all get out, but I know he didn't (a) understand, (b) want to understand, or (c) feel the need to understand why issues of racial justice under the umbrella of social justice were important. So we have some folks who would fall under that category of 'I just want to teach my science methods course,' which he saw as sort of race neutral."

In contrast, the willingness to engage the emotional component of dismantling racism sets RJP instructors apart from others who simply teach required methods or content courses. RJP faculty move beyond a transmission model to a desire to transform teachers' deeply held beliefs. They engage in critical self-reflection about Whiteness, how to navigate and push in affirming ways, and how to engage in their own self-care. Fujiyoshi describes the challenge of creating warm relationships with students, particularly White students who are resisting or have a lot of need for validation: "We're trying to talk about building relationships [in our classes] and the importance of having warmth in the classroom, and then I'm caught in this conundrum where I am not doing that with you. But wait, I still have to model this so let me take a step back." Fujiyoshi makes the commitment to the work by stepping back, reflecting, and pushing herself to continue to build the trusting relationships for students to grow.

Shortly after our interview, Pour-Khorshid sent me an article titled "I Was Wrong to Tell You to De-Center Your Feelings, White People," written by April Dawn Harter, LCSW, a Black anti-racist therapist.[7] Pour-Khorshid explained what appealed to her about the article: "I keep thinking about how it takes a certain type/level of emotional labor that may not be for everyone to do, but as I specifically think about this as a racial justice/healing justice facilitator in particular, I think we do need more effective ways of doing this work and having these conversations and supporting understanding, healing, growth, change." While it is grueling, Villarreal explains her take on when students have breakthroughs: "I don't think I could still be doing this every day if I didn't see people in those moments."

WHAT ARE THE SPACES IN WHICH TEACHER
EDUCATION CAN ADVANCE RACIAL JUSTICE?

The previous sections described how RJPs structure themselves programmatically. This section looks at the pedagogical spaces for engaging racial justice as candidates begin their journey through the programs. I will not go into detail about the specific assignments and syllabi of the RJPs here; rather, I will summarize the goals of coursework and then describe the different programmatic structures of learning in which racial justice is integrated.

To briefly summarize the goal of coursework in an RJP: The courses are designed to teach topics typically included in teacher education such as methods and content, but this is done while allowing students to reframe their understanding of race across racial justice frameworks such as the Four I's of Oppression and Advantage. Pour-Khorshid describes this in the UESJ program: "This is a program committed to social justice, which means you are going to have to unpack your racial identity. Not just your racial identity; you're going to have to be unpacking the various forms of privilege and power that you hold." Both Pour-Khorshid and Villarreal are also trained facilitators with Flourish Agenda, a national nonprofit that provides Radical Healing Workshops, which they have brought into their respective programs. Pour-Khorshid explains:

> We use Shawn Ginwright's framework of healing-centered engagement that argues that to aim toward social justice, we need to heal from oppression at various levels. So we're looking at the individual kind of harm we've experienced under the oppression that we live in, in society. But then we're also trying to heal interpersonal relationships, the ways we engage with our students, the ways we engage with our families, the ways we engage with

our communities. Ultimately we're also trying to heal institutions because we understand that institutions are shaped by oppression and perpetuate harm.[8]

Pour-Khorshid illuminates how all of the Four I's are interconnected and are addressed as part of her RJP. The following section examines all of the spaces, in addition to coursework, where the RJPs rely on the humanizing relationships they have developed to further their racial justice goals.

ORGANIZE STUDENTS INTO COHORTS

Once programs select students with the most potential to become critically conscious, anti-racist teachers, RJPs organize students in ways that develop the kinds of humanizing communities that build the trust for racial justice work. Every one of the RJPs in this chapter used a cohort model. Cohorts are small groups of students placed together for the scope and sequence of their coursework and fieldwork. While not exclusive to RJPs, traditional programs often have large numbers of candidates, and it becomes more efficient for students to register for classes that fit their individual schedules, rather than try to coordinate them into particular groupings that meet together. The benefit of cohorts, however, is that they allow students to have a community of peers in which to build relationships, share experiences, reflect on new knowledge and feelings, and engage in challenging conversations. For advancing racial justice, the cohorts become a space where the work is furthered through peer discussion, and it can be particularly powerful when the cohorts are made up of racially diverse candidates with different life experiences.

While each RJP is structured differently in terms of how much time and when in the program sequence students are in their cohorts, each uses the cohort as a home place for key experiences and learning. Fujiyoshi reflects on some of the benefits of the cohort as a space to address racial justice: "It's a great bonding experience for the cohort. It creates moments to really grow together, to be vulnerable, to listen, to empathize, to express compassion, but also to call things out. To be shocked, to be pissed."

By building relationships in cohorts, opportunities for cross-racial dialogues support greater awareness and understanding across difference. Annamarie Francois said, "What's important for us is that they learn together side by side and that they have courageous conversations with one another, because by separating them, the conversation is going to stay safe, particularly for our White students, and we don't want that." As she implied, the mixed-race nature of these dialogues pushes the students, particularly the White students, to understand their future role in classrooms with students of Color. "We're really trying to push the envelope and transform the way we talk to one another about teaching, the way we understand the students that we're serving, and the way that our identities impact that."

Because the RJPs prioritize admitting candidates of Color, the White students are often the minority within their cohorts. This creates opportunities for learning from people of Color that many White students have never had. As Howard explains, "In our courses, unlike most other programs in the country, White students are in the minority. And I think that dynamic lends itself to a host of different things that happened in terms of the interactions." Maloney expanded on what some of those different things are for the White students: "They are learning to teach in an environment that is intended for teachers of Color, so they are learning perspectives and hearing perspectives that they have not likely heard—certainly not fronted in other aspects of their teacher education."

She believes that because of this, "those particular teachers are going to be mindful of race in ways that I don't think they would have been."

These mixed-race cohorts allow students to learn from their different experiences when topics of race are made explicit. For example, Maloney described a racial autobiography that our candidates wrote and shared with each other. "We were able to talk about how we all were experiencing race differently based upon our racial background. And so students started to realize, particularly the White students, 'Oh, everybody didn't have the same experiences as me!' But also I wanted them to think about how your experiences have given you a false sense of what is normal." In examples such as this, the mixed-race cohorts allow all students to learn from each other's positionality. While the mixed-race cohorts provide these opportunities, they often happen because of the emotional labor of people of Color. Because of this, many RJPs have also created racial affinity spaces so that both groups have room to be themselves and do the appropriate work and healing for their communities.

CREATE RACIAL AFFINITY SPACES

Also referred to as *identity caucusing*, racial affinity groups provide a space for White people and people of Color to separately explore the impact of the Four I's, particularly internalized racial inferiority and superiority. This allows people in both groups to be bravely honest, to stumble and say the wrong thing, and to move forward while minimizing cross-racial harm.

The program at USF is just starting to implement racial affinity spaces within their student teaching course; the groups meet a few times a semester. Pour-Khorshid explained how the spaces further candidates' theoretical understandings of race: "What does it mean when we talk about Whiteness? There's this assumption that just because a reading is assigned that the students 'get it' and that they've grappled with it and are now ready to act accordingly, which is not the case. I think there's a lot of intentional reflection that needs to happen." In order to create the space for this intentional reflection, the student teaching course is implementing the affinity groups so "that process is not at the expense of the students of Color. . . . So we are offering different kinds of entry points to the theory [of Whiteness] and then having them come back into the racial affinity spaces and have structured protocols around unpacking what they heard, what they resonated with, what were things that were challenging, and why."

For students of Color, racial affinity groups provide a reprieve from White people and the harm they can often inflict when bumbling through learning about racism in cross-racial groups. It also provides a space for students of Color to unpack how they are impacted by the Four I's of Oppression, particularly how they have internalized racism and how they may be unconsciously upholding Whiteness. In our emerging work with racial affinity groups in NTP, we offer three groups based on how students identify: one for White students, one for Black students, and one for non-Black students of Color. In the White group, I lead the students to break the silence about race and discuss various ways we uphold Whiteness. Maloney facilitates the group for Black students, and conversations have focused on both Black joy as well as internalized oppression. In our group for non-Black students of Color, we have invited a colleague, Blanca Vega at MSU, as well as Pour-Khorshid and Villarreal, to facilitate, and their discussions have centered on how anti-Blackness lives in their communities.

PROVIDE ONE-ON-ONE MEETINGS

The racial affinity spaces provide a place for students to collectively work out issues stemming from their racial identity development. Most of the RJPs also do this work with individual candidates privately. Because of the commitment to creating humanizing experiences, the RJPs recognize how personal much of this work is. In order to attend to the individual process that students work through in their development as anti-racist educators, many of the RJPs build opportunities to have one-on-one meetings with students. Fujiyoshi further demonstrates how these relationships create the space for the necessary work of dismantling Whiteness. "I try to meet with everybody at least once during that quarter to talk about their process of seeing themselves. It sometimes brings up stuff that people just haven't addressed before. I'm not asking anybody to dig into the vault, but I think in some ways people want to."

Fujiyoshi recognizes that she is asking students to be vulnerable, but that the meetings are purposeful. "Those one-on-one meetings are really where our students end up talking through their own wrestling, their own investigation. And sometimes there are really tough ways that they just need a little support. It really gets us at a place where we can think about what it means to be human—and I think being human right now is pretty tough. I think that's why it's very emotional. It can be very heavy at times."

One-on-ones can provide an additional space to disrupt Whiteness or support students who are hitting bumps in the road of their racial development. When White faculty lead these meetings with White students, one-on-ones can also be a strategy for alleviating some of the emotional toll endured by students and faculty of Color. Kennedy recalled a White student who kept enacting his Whiteness in ways that were inappropriate and harmful toward his peers of Color in his cohort. The student had received the message that as a White man, he needed to position himself as a learner. But he overcorrected this message and ended up frustrating his cohort members who felt he was relying on them as people of Color to teach him about racism. Kennedy remembered his confusion and agitation in trying to do Whiteness "right." Kennedy used the opportunity for a one-on-one to support this student's development. "He didn't get it at all. . . . He had like this huge breakdown, where he was yelling and storming around the office. It just took time, it took conversation, and just the trust that I built with him for him to understand that he was also still doing something that was problematic—expecting other people to teach him."

As another White man, Kennedy recognized the importance of this space for the student to work these emotions out so as not to put it on his cohort members of Color. "It's exhausting work, and he needs to go out and do that work on his own. Part of that work is what he was doing in that moment with me. That's where he should be taking that energy and time." Kennedy created space to remove the burden of working through Whiteness from the students of Color. He continued: "So, then he went back to the cohort with this new learning in a way that was still a little self-congratulatory, but with a real perspective of how he doesn't have to just constantly be like, 'Teach me that.' There are things that he can learn, that he can contribute, and he can make mistakes in ways that are not actually harmful."

Finally, one-on-ones can also support students who are advancing in their racial consciousness and are ready to take on more than the rest of the cohort may be ready for. Pour-Khorshid described a White student who was frustrated in class by her more resistant White peers. "She checked in with me afterward, and after that very long conversation, I feel like she's just been constantly checking in with me. She'll ask me for different resources, or she'll ask me what I think about certain things. I think it's been really on her mind since she has been exposed, so now she's able to see it and feel safe enough to talk to me about it." By building on the trusting relationships fostered in the RJPs, one-on-ones provide a space of differentiated support based on where individual students are within their journeys toward racial justice.

ENGAGE WITH THE COMMUNITY

While all teacher education programs have requirements for students to spend time in the field or schools and communities, traditional efforts often could be described as poverty tourism. Candidates become spectators in urban communities, viewing the pain of poverty and institutional racism, with no analysis of the forces that have looted such communities. This results in reinforcing deficit thinking about urban areas, rather than understanding the assets, resistance, resilience, and heart of such communities. Many students try to avoid teaching in urban schools, and in fact, several interviewees shared stories of undergraduates' parents who called trying to plead for their child's safety in an attempt to get them out of an urban placement. When such students are "forced" into these placements without a systemic analysis, they often see the challenges urban communities face as the residents' own fault. For example, they complain about the condition of the neighborhood without understanding its lack of municipal services. In traditional programs, the university supervisors may share these deficit views and are therefore not positioned to interrupt or transform such conceptualizations.

In contrast, RJPs are intentional about engaging with local communities in ways that are reciprocal and that explicitly address the Four I's. The UTEP program in Chicago has a robust approach to community engagement in which their candidates spend a great deal of time working in specific grassroots organizations run by and for people of Color. Their goal is for candidates to build relationships with the community organizers and also to understand the history of Chicago. Fujiyoshi asked, "How do we understand the makeup of Chicago when we're looking at the conditions of schooling? We have to take into consideration the political economy and racial segregation. So we're working with organizations that have that community knowledge." It is through these relationships that candidates gain knowledge and reframe institutional and interpersonal racism. Fujiyoshi continues:

> I think some students don't actually ever have connections or relationships with people of Color outside of working in a school . . . where there's a power dynamic between them and kids of Color. Serving as an intern with a community organization that's led by people of Color that are from the communities that are also really about self-determination . . . just the tenacity of these organizations, but also their heart, is what really is important for our students to engage with. To be able to see communities in a different way, that these aren't places that need you to come and fix. There are already people working within these communities that have had a history of working in the community, that have had a history of organizing and community activism that was happening long before you.

Fujiyoshi recognizes that by engaging in these communities, White candidates can reframe some of their missionary tendencies. "Before you come in thinking, 'I need to come and save this place, these children need me,' take a step back for a second and see who already is here, what's already being done, and really think about yourself in terms of your allyship. The philosophy that we hear from our organizations is solidarity, not charity."

Similarly, Center X structures community engagement into their coursework as an opportunity to develop an assets-based approach that positions people from local communities as experts rather than people in need of help. Francois explains that right from the beginning of coursework, candidates are "walking in a community with elders to talk about the history of the community, they are doing home visits, they're taking photographs and mapping the assets." These activities support students to realize they are not the experts. "They're not making determinations about the neighborhood themselves, they're asking folks. They're asking the gas station attendant, the person at the laundromat, 'Tell me about your neighborhood, tell me about this school. What are your hopes and your dreams for the school?'"

This experience helps candidates recognize the importance of entering a space with humility and with an understanding that they are not the experts. Francois insists that "to identify the wealth and the needs of a community—that has to come from the people who live there." Because this community engagement happens early in the program, she encourages candidates to "use that information throughout your methods courses and throughout your other courses to inform the formal content that you are learning and to recognize that the problems lie not in the community." This community engagement element of the RJPs allows students to build relationships and access knowledge that helps them reframe their understandings of all Four I's.

CONTINUE SUPPORT AFTER GRADUATION

While the RJPs work hard to advance racial justice from admissions to graduation, they recognize that a year or two of teacher education is not enough time to reframe a lifetime of racial socialization while simultaneously preparing someone for the technical aspects of teaching. As such, many of the programs broaden their relationship with their students' post-graduation into a period referred to as induction, when new teachers are entering the field. Through induction support, which sometimes involves critical professional development sessions or in-classroom mentorship, RJPs are able to extend their racial justice reach. The time spent fostering humanizing relationships and trust early in the program often flourishes as these long-term relationships develop. For example, while there is only one year of the official RJP at University of Chicago, they provide multiple years of induction support, so alumni remain very much part of the daily conversation. Fujiyoshi explains:

> I say five years, because at a staff meeting, for instance, we're still talking about people from three years ago, four years ago, five years ago. So they're still on our radar, but they're not officially in our program. We want to hear about our students from our coaches. We want to hear about who's doing awesome, who is struggling during what and why, and could we have seen that.

By creating coherence between what happened in initial coursework and induction support, the racial justice perspectives taught previously are more likely to find their way into classroom practice. Kennedy explained that at UTEP, candidates are prepared to know that induction coaches are going to be engaging them in critical conversations using a racial justice lens. He says:

> This is the lens we're applying to all the situations that you're having. We're going to talk about it and we're going to connect it back to what you read in that first year, because if those ideas just sit in a folder somewhere and they're not part of your daily practice, then

you're just going to fall out of routine, especially because you're going to be socialized into these school environments where that's just not the case.

As Kennedy alludes, once they are in schools, teachers will be held accountable to innumerable standards, but it is unlikely that racial justice will be one of them.

Francois also works to address this challenge through induction: "We continue to provide them with field support because we know that once they get into these schools, they may not have the leadership that believes in justice the way we do. They've been trained to think of race a particular way, and they're willing to engage in a hard conversation." Francois recognizes that there may be a disconnect between this training and what happens when they become teachers in a school that doesn't share this justice stance. "But then you have a school, and a leader at the school, where it is not okay to stand in that [justice stance], so we continue to work with them through their first year of teaching. We're in schools. We're in their classrooms every other week keeping them focused."

While some of the work is with the new teachers, helping them stay connected to their justice-minded aspirations, other times the work is about preparing the school leadership to understand the teachers' racial justice lens and practices. Francois explains: "I'm working with the principal to help them understand why this young [teacher] is taking so much time developing community in their classroom. Why is this young [teacher] bringing real-life problems into the classroom? Why do we have the students outside addressing the issues in their community and then looking at it through the lens of content?" The RJPs recognize that it is unfair to throw new anti-racist teachers into the field without extending this lifeline. "I feel like that's part of our responsibility as teacher educators, that we don't just prepare them. You gotta support them in arguably the most difficult year, the year outside of teacher preparation."

Many of the faculty in these RJPs, including myself, are affiliated with local and national social justice education organizations that actively work on issues of racial justice. Across the country, there is a loose network called Teacher Activist Groups made up of local organizations such as Teachers 4 Social Justice in San Francisco; People's Education Movement in Los Angeles, Oakland, and Chicago; Teachers for Social Justice in Chicago; New York Collective of Radical Educators (NYCoRE) in New York City; TAG Philly and TAG Boston; along with national groups such as the Education for Liberation Network. Many of these organizations have racial affinity groups, host annual conferences, and organize around issues such as the school-to-prison pipeline and high-stakes testing, among others.

Because RJP faculty have relationships with such groups, either as members or supporters, they create opportunities within their programs for students to become involved in these networks, allowing them to realize that they are part of something bigger. As a former student of mine once expressed after attending a NYCoRE conference, "Before, if I didn't like something, I'd go, 'Well, that sucks,' and I didn't realize that other people think it sucks too and we can all get together and do something." Either by bringing teacher activists in as guest speakers or by having students attend the organizations' conferences and events, students in RJPs learn that there are other educators outside of their cohort committed to racial justice. As students graduate and become classroom teachers, these organizations become places for them to find co-conspirators and avenues for racial justice activism.

CONCLUSION

Throughout this book, I have emphasized the relationship among the various levels of the Four I's of Oppression and Advantage. In the opening, I explained that one of the reasons that #CurriculumSoWhite proliferates is because an *individual* teacher's problematic understandings of race are amplified through their *institutional* power. In the following chapters, I argued that a strategy for dismantling #CurriculumSoWhite is actually through the inverse relationship of institutional and individual racism. These two closing chapters about the RJPs demonstrate that through transforming the *institution* of teacher education, there is opportunity to disrupt *individual* preservice teachers' racial *ideology* prior to their entering the classroom. These teachers will still wield institutional power, but they will do so with reframed understandings of race and with the desire to work toward anti-racism rather than to uphold structures of White supremacy.

In the introduction, I claimed that #CurriculumSoWhite is especially nefarious because rather than operating at just the teacher's individual level, it maintains Whiteness on all four levels: ideological, institutional, interpersonal, and internalized. By restructuring teacher education to transform teachers' understandings toward anti-racism, teachers now have the potential to instead disrupt Whiteness at all four levels.

When teacher education programs are structured to interrupt teachers' mainstream understanding of race, programs are positioned to go beyond just changing the lesson plans aspiring teachers might teach. The RJPs demonstrate that in addition to disrupting curricular Tools of Whiteness, transformations can happen at multiple levels. First, racial justice programs become places with a unified ideology, creating a tight-knit community with a shared mission—along with institutional power—committed to racial justice in schools. Such programs are able to transform the racial consciousness of preservice teachers, both White and people of Color, alongside committed mentors, supervisors, and faculty associated with these programs.

The individual aspiring teachers who attend RJPs have had the opportunity to reframe their racial ideologies to focus on anti-racism. Next, they enter K–12 schools with the commitment and skills to apply their racial justice frame, thus potentially transforming those institutions. Importantly, children in these schools benefit from these anti-racist educators because they will not be subjected to the trauma of #CurriculumSoWhite and will instead be taught in humanizing and culturally sustaining ways.[9] Finally, when teachers are able to recognize their Tools of Whiteness and the damage it causes, they can join the families in chapter 1 in pushing back against racist pedagogy, potentially transforming the production of curriculum.

Unfortunately, RJPs are the exception to how teacher education functions, not the rule. Many programs exist with little or superficial attention to racial justice, focusing instead on approaches such as multiculturalism or cultural competence that develop specific pedagogical strategies without transforming underlying foundations of racist ideology. Therefore, many aspiring teachers are not provided the opportunity to transform their socialized understandings of race prior to entering K–12 schools, priming them to inflict egregious acts of curricular violence through their own #CurriculumSoWhite.

But by scaling up and sustaining the practices in RJPs, the broader field of teacher preparation has the potential to become a serious threat to the maintenance of racism in schools. It requires similar efforts in recruiting and developing not just teachers but also teacher educators with the commitment and capacity to work toward anti-racism. But ultimately, by transforming teacher education into spaces dedicated to racial justice, we can have an institutional response that preemptively interrupts the norm of reading, writing, and racism in schools. These RJPs provide a path toward the radical possibilities of what humanizing education can look like in teacher education and in schools.

ACKNOWLEDGMENTS

To me, writing a book feels like submitting a final paper for a course, summing up what I have learned about racism and Whiteness up until the point of publication. As I get ready to turn this particular final in, the ultimate acknowledgement goes to my teachers. I am so grateful for the lessons and mentorship that I have received and continue to receive from the great Bonnie Billups, Carrie Secret, Suzanne Carothers, and Jennifer Robinson. You have shaped my way of being in the world, and I am ever grateful for your generosity, investment, and trust in me. As all great teachers, you helped develop my lens and cleared a path for me to do the work. Thank you.

Writing this particular book involved thorny, ongoing wrestling with my identity and a re-imagining of accountability. Thank you for being on this journey with me and for your unwavering, critical love and sisterhood, Rosa Rivera-McCutchen, Tanya Maloney, Christina Villarreal, and Anne Marie Marshall. I am so grateful for the comradeship and love of Farima Pour-Khorshid, Edward Curammeng, and Carolina Valdez and Naiara.

To say that I am a member of a community of unwavering passion for justice would be an understatement. I am forever grateful to be part of this educational justice family, and this book is only possible because of our shared vision, work, and community. There are many of us, but specific appreciation goes to Lauren Adams and Marylin Zuniga, Denisse Andrade and Seth Radar and Camino, Awo Okaikor Ayree-Price, Wayne Au, Patrick Camangian, Stephanie Cariaga, Keith Catone and Dulari Tahbildar and Ishaan, Emily Clark and Alanna Howe and Maeve and Tessa, Cyrene Crooms, Cati de los Ríos and Roger Viet Chung and Taiyari and Miguelito, Maddy Fox and Sam Coleman and Rex and Anya, Rosie Frascella and Cristina Marie Hilo and Niki Malaya, Daren Graves, Akiea Gross, Sharim Hannegan-Martinez, Rita Kamani-Renedo, Harper Keenan, Kari Kokka, Kevin Kumashiro, Jamila Lyiscott, Justis Lopez, Ariana Mangual Figueroa and Ben Lerner and Lucía and Marcela, Edwin Mayorga and Jen Lee with Teo and Juju, Oscar Navarro, Thomas Nikundiwe and Carla Shalaby, Natalia Ortiz, Aja Reynolds, Masiel Rodriguez-Vars, Camika Royal, Yolanda Sealey-Ruiz, Tammy Spencer, David Stovall, Monica White, and Karen Zapata.

Becoming part of the Beacon Press family allowed this book to find a home with people who are also committed to racial justice. Thank you Bill and Rick Ayers for bringing me to the front door and for mentoring me throughout my academic career. What a wonderful experience it was to work with my sharp and endlessly patient editor, Rachael Marks. The book became tighter with every round of feedback from Lisa Bethel, Adam Hochschuler, Susan Lumenello, William Waters, Nancy Walser, and Christina Villarreal. Thank you for the careful read and feedback from Robin DiAngelo, Eve Ewing, Carla Shalaby, and Sonia Nieto. I'm incredibly humbled and honored that the brilliant Bettina Love graced this book with a foreword. The latter part of this book has been shaped by experiences and insights from numerous people, and I thank you for sharing your knowledge and experiences: Patrick Camangian, Casey Doyle, AnnaMarie Francois, Sarah Frydlewicz, Kay Fujiyoshi, Tyrone

Howard, Bill Kennedy, Tanya Maloney, Farima Pour-Khorshid, and Maria Suto.

I am fortunate to have received a sabbatical from Montclair State University to work on this book and am grateful for the ongoing community and support from my dean, Tamara Lucas, and my colleagues, including Jessica Bacon, Maria Cioé Peña, Naome Dunnell and TJ, Chase and Chance, Carolina Gonzalez, Sumi Hagawari, Priya Lalvani, Kimi Santos, Rebecca Swann-Jackson, Blanca Vega, and Mayida Zaal and Imani.

The most exciting part of my job is watching as my teacher education students become inspirational teachers who bring a vision of racial and social justice alive in their classrooms. This joy of staying in community with alumni/ae has taken on new meaning when we begin working shoulder to shoulder in the struggle for justice—your dedication and purpose keeps me inspired and engaged Marylin Zuniga, Nelly Bess, Cariesha Black, Jasmine Johnson, Elisa Lee, Tatiana Pererya, Carla Nisbett, and Jackie Santos. I'm proud to watch you continue to grow in your justice stance: Michele Bernadino, Veronica Cueva, Becky Erdelyi, Amanda Faison, Lisa Fishman, Brenda Huacachino, Jackie Keenan, Gianna LaBanca, Nicole Larsen, Megan McBride, Elizabeth Mojica, Rouxana Pellicier, Jessica Rivera, Rebekah and Pablo de la Rosa, Cristiana Sardo, Debbie Schultz, Claire Thomas, Jorge Villacreses, Haley Yacos, and the entire 2020 cohort of the Newark Teacher Project, whom I love dearly.

As always, I am grateful first and foremost to Mom for your lifelong support. And to my family: David Dahn, Kristine Larsen and Django and Roxxy Gilligan, David and Natalija Marshall, Al McCutchen and Elliott, Najah and Anayah Rivera-McCutchen, Chris Powers, Anna Sop, Martika, Chaka, and Frankie.

NOTES

FOREWORD

1. kihana miraya ross, "Call It What It Is: Anti-Blackness," op-ed, *New York Times*, June 4, 2020.

INTRODUCTION: #CURRICULUMSOWHITE

1. W. E. B. Du Bois, *Darkwater: Voices from Within the Veil* (New York: Harcourt, Brace and Howe, 1920), 31.

2. Django Paris, "There's #OscarsSoWhite and Then There's #CurriculumSoWhite How Curriculum in US Public Schools Remains Centered on White Middleclass Norms," Twitter post, January 29, 2016, https://twitter.com/django_paris/status/693138673894854656.

3. David Whisenant, "School System Apologizes for 'Inappropriate' Homework Assignment," WBTV, December 10, 2019, https://www.wbtv.com/2019/12/10/school-system-apologizes-inappropriate-homework-assignment.

4. Michael Harriot, "Could You List the 'Positive Aspects' of Slavery? A Teacher Asked 8th-Graders to Do So," *Root*, April 20, 2018, https://www.theroot.com/could-you-list-the-positive-aspects-of-slavery-a-tea-1825430656.

5. Zahara Hill, "Bronx Teacher Steps on Backs of Black Students in Slavery 'Lesson,'" *Ebony*, February 2, 2018, https://www.ebony.com/news/bronx-teacher-slavery-lesson.

6. E. Brown, "Texas Officials: Schools Should Teach That Slavery Was 'Side Issue' to Civil War," July 5, 2015, https://www.washingtonpost.com/local/education/150-years-later-schools-are-still-a-battlefield-for

-interpreting-civil-war/2015/07/05/e8fbd57e-2001–11e5-bf41-c23f5d3face
1_story.html.

7. Michael Schaub, "Do New Texas Textbooks Whitewash Slavery and
Segregation?," *Los Angeles Times*, July 7, 2015, https://www.latimes.com
/books/jacketcopy/la-et-jc-do-new-texas-textbooks-whitewash-slavery
-segregation-20150707-story.html.

8. Carter Godwin Woodson, *The Mis-Education of the Negro* (Wash-
ington, DC: Associated Publishers, 1933); Gloria Ladson-Billings, *Critical
Race Theory Perspectives on the Social Studies: The Profession, Policies,
and Curriculum* (Charlotte, NC: Information Age Publishing, 2003);
James W. Loewen, *Lies My Teacher Told Me: Everything Your American
History Textbook Got Wrong* (New York: New Press, 2008); Eve Tuck and
Rubén A. Gaztambide-Fernández, "Curriculum, Replacement, and Settler
Futurity," *Journal of Curriculum Theorizing* 29, no. 1 (June 18, 2013): 72,
http://journal.jctonline.org/index.php/jct/article/view/411; Dolores Calderon, "Uncovering Settler Grammars in Curriculum," *Educational Studies*
50, no. 4 (July 4, 2014): 313–38, https://doi.org/10.1080/00131946.2014.926
904; Prentice T. Chandler, *Doing Race in Social Studies: Critical Perspectives*
(Charlotte, NC: Information Age Publishing, 2015); Anthony L. Brown
and Keffrelyn D. Brown, "The More Things Change, the More They Stay
the Same: Excavating Race and the Enduring Racisms in U.S. Curriculum," *Teachers College Record* 117, no. 14 (2015): 103–30; LaGarrett J. King,
Perspectives of Black Histories in Schools (Charlotte, NC: Information Age
Publishing, 2019).

9. Adrienne Green, "More Minority Students, Fewer Teachers of
Color," *Atlantic*, September 2015, http://www.theatlantic.com/education
/archive/2015/09/teacher-diversity-viz/406033.

10. Rebecca Goldring, Lucinda Gray, and Amy Bitterman, *Characteristics of Public and Private Elementary and Secondary School Teachers in
the United States: Results from the 2011–12 Schools and Staffing Survey First
Look* (Washington, DC: National Center for Education Statistics, 2013),
eric.ed.gov/?id=ED544178.

11. ACT, Inc., *The Condition of Future Educators 2015* (2016), https://
www.act.org/content/dam/act/unsecured/documents/Future-Educators
-2015.pdf.

12. H. Richard Milner and Tyrone C. Howard, "Counter-Narrative as
Method: Race, Policy and Research for Teacher Education," *Race Ethnicity
and Education* 16, no. 4 (September 26, 2013): 536–61, https://doi.org/10.10
80/13613324.2013.817772.

13. To further knowledge and understanding of how racism functions
in American society, these are some good places to start: *The New Jim
Crow: Mass Incarceration in the Age of Colorblindness* (New York: New
Press, 2010), by Michelle Alexander; *White Rage: The Unspoken Truth of*

Our Racial Divide (New York: Bloomsbury, 2016), by Carol Anderson; *Killing Rage: Ending Racism* (New York: Henry Holt, 1996), by bell hooks; *An Indigenous Peoples' History of the United States* (Boston: Beacon Press, 2015), by Roxanne Dunbar-Ortiz; *Stamped from the Beginning: The Definitive History of Racist Ideas in America* (New York: Nation Books, 2016), by Ibram X. Kendi; *My Grandmother's Hands: Racialized Trauma and the Pathway to Mending Our Hearts and Bodies* (Las Vegas: Central Recovery Press, 2017), by Resmaa Menakem; *Race: The Power of an Illusion*, a 2003 film by California Newsreel, https://www.racepowerofanillusion.org/; *So You Want to Talk About Race* (New York: Seal Press, 2019), by Ijeoma Oluo; *An African American and Latinx History of the United States* (Boston: Beacon Press, 2018), by Paul Ortiz; and *Just Mercy: A Story of Justice and Redemption* (New York: Spiegel & Grau, 2015), by Bryan Stevenson. To further your understanding about how racism operates specifically in education, these are important texts: *Teaching/Learning Anti-Racism* (New York: Teachers College Press, 1997), by Louise Derman-Sparks and Carol Brunson Phillips; *Ghosts in the Schoolyard: Racism and School Closings on Chicago's South Side* (Chicago: University of Chicago Press, 2020), by Eve Ewing; *We Want to Do More Than Survive: Abolitionist Teaching and the Pursuit of Educational Freedom* (Boston: Beacon Press, 2019), by Bettina Love; *Black Appetite. White Food: Issues of Race, Voice, and Justice Within and Beyond the Classroom* (New York: Routledge, 2019), by Jamila Lyiscott; *Everyday Antiracism: Getting Real About Race in School* (New York: New Press, 2008), by Mica Pollack; *Born Out of Struggle: Critical Race Theory, School Creation, and the Politics of Interruption* (Albany: SUNY Press, 2016), by David Stovall; and *Why Are All the Black Kids Sitting Together in the Cafeteria?* (New York: BasicBooks, 1997), by Beverly Daniel Tatum.

14. Stuart Hall, "The Problem of Ideology-Marxism without Guarantees," *Journal of Communication Inquiry* 10, no. 2 (June 1986): 18, https://doi.org/10.1177/019685998601000203, 26.

15. Robert Jensen, *The Heart of Whiteness: Confronting Race, Racism, and White Privilege* (San Francisco: City Lights, 2005), 4.

16. Joe L. Kincheloe and Shirley R. Steinberg, *Changing Multiculturalism* (Buckingham, UK: Open University Press, 1997), 83.

17. Eduardo Bonilla-Silva, *Racism Without Racists: Color-Blind Racism and the Persistence of Racial Inequality in the United States* (Lanham, MD: Rowman & Littlefield, 2010); Gloria Ladson-Billings, *Crossing Over to Canaan: The Journey of New Teachers in Diverse Classrooms* (San Francisco: Jossey-Bass, 2001), 81; Tatum, *Why Are All the Black Kids Sitting Together in the Cafeteria?*

18. For White people interested in examining the ways we personally enact Whiteness, I recommend *Me and White Supremacy: Combat Racism, Change the World, and Become a Good Ancestor* (Naperville,

IL: Sourcebooks, 2020), a workbook by Layla F. Saad, alongside *White Fragility: Why It's So Hard for White People to Talk About Racism* (Boston: Beacon Press, 2018), by Robin DiAngelo; *Whiteness as Property* (Cambridge, MA: Harvard Law Review Association, 1993), by Cheryl Harris; *We Can't Teach What We Don't Know: White Teachers, Multiracial Schools* (New York: Teachers College Press, 2016), by Gary R. Howard; *Feeling White: Whiteness, Emotionality, and Education* (Netherlands: Sense, 2016), by Cheryl E. Matias; and *This Book Is Anti-Racist: 20 Lessons on How to Wake Up, Take Action, and Do the Work* (Minneapolis: Quarto, 2020), by Tiffany Jewell.

19. Andrea Ayvazian et al., *Dismantling Racism: 2016 Workbook* (DismantlingRacism.org, 2018), https://resourcegeneration.org/wp-content/uploads/2018/01/2016-dRworks-workbook.pdf. This workbook is designed to be used with the Dismantling Racism workshop and provides descriptions, along with "antidotes" for each of these aspects of White supremacist culture. It also provides a rich collection of anti-racism training activities.

20. Sherry Marx and Julie Pennington, "Pedagogies of Critical Race Theory: Experimentations with White Preservice Teachers," *International Journal of Qualitative Studies in Education* 16 (January 1, 2003): 101, https://doi.org/10.1080/0951839022000036381.

21. Critical race scholars in the field of education include Gloria Ladson-Billings, William F. Tate, Marvin Lynn, Daniel Solorzano, David Stovall, and Tara J. Yosso.

22. Derrick Bell, *Faces at the Bottom of the Well: The Permanence of Racism* (New York: Basic Books, 1992).

23. Kendi, *Stamped from the Beginning.*

24. Like all terms used to describe social categories, language shifts and changes over time. These articles explain some of the issues surrounding such terms as *people of Color* and *BIPOC.* Constance Grady, "The Meaning of BIPOC, as Explained by Linguists," *Vox,* June 30, 2020, https://www.vox.com/2020/6/30/21300294/bipoc-what-does-it-mean-critical-race-linguistics-jonathan-rosa-deandra-miles-hercules; Sandra E. Garcia, "BIPOC: What Does It Mean?," *New York Times,* June 17, 2020, https://www.nytimes.com/article/what-is-bipoc.html.

25. Anne Bonds and Joshua Inwood, "Beyond White Privilege: Geographies of White Supremacy and Settler Colonialism," *Progress in Human Geography* 40, no. 6 (December 10, 2016): 715–33, https://doi.org/10.1177/0309132515613166.

26. For a short, user-friendly overview of the Four I's, see Eliana Pipes, "Legos and the 4 I's of Oppression," July 29, 2016, https://www.youtube.com/watch?v=3WWyVRo4Uas.

27. James A. Banks, *An Introduction to Multicultural Education* (Boston: Allyn and Bacon, 1999).

28. Yolanda Sealey-Ruiz, "The Archaeology of the Self," NYU Metro Center, December 7, 2018, https://www.youtube.com/watch?v=OwC_3c LRJO8.

29. Edwin Mayorga and Bree Picower, "Active Solidarity: Centering the Demands and Vision of the Black Lives Matter Movement in Teacher Education," *Urban Education* 53, no. 2 (December 20, 2017): 212–30, https://doi.org/10.1177/0042085917747117.

30. Laura Bult, "Alabama Middle School Causes Outrage for Handing Out Math Quiz with Blatant Gang References," *New York Daily News*, June 1, 2016, http://www.nydailynews.com/news/national/alabama-middle -school-teacher-put-leave-gang-math-test-article-1.2656876.

31. I write in more detail about the specifics of my personal journey in my first book, *Practice What You Teach*. Bree Picower, *Practice What You Teach: Social Justice Education in the Classroom and the Streets* (New York: Routledge, 2012).

32. John R. Rickford and Russell J. Rickford, *Spoken Soul: The Story of Black English* (New York: Wiley, 2000); Theresa Perry, Claude Steele, and Asa G. Hilliard, *Young, Gifted, and Black: Promoting High Achievement Among African-American Students* (Boston: Beacon Press, 2003).

33. Alicia Garza, "A Herstory of the #BlackLivesMatter Movement," Resist, June 16, 2015, https://resist.org/news/herstory-blacklivesmatter -movement.

34. Sweeney Kovar, "Macklemore—White Privilege II (Ft. Jamila Woods)," Indie Shuffle, January 24, 2016, https://www.indieshuffle.com /macklemore-white-privilege-ii-ft-jamila-woods.

35. Bettina L. Love, *We Want to Do More Than Survive: Abolitionist Teaching and the Pursuit of Educational Freedom* (Boston: Beacon Press, 2019).

36. "White people should NOT be capitalizing . . . ," Ericka Hart, @iHartEricka, September 18, 2019, Twitter, https://twitter.com/ihartericka /status/1174447440344375296.

37. Sonya Renee Taylor, "Should White Folks Get Paid to Do Anti-Racism Work?," Instagram, September 20, 2019, https://www.instagram .com/tv/B2oiB4zgVIs.

38. Tre Johnson, "When Black People Are in Pain, White People Just Join Book Clubs," *Washington Post*, June 11, 2020, https://www.washington post.com/outlook/white-antiracist-allyship-book-clubs/2020/06/11/9edcc766 -abf5-11ea-94d2-d7bc43b26bf9_story.html.

39. Marisa Meltzer, "'I Refuse to Listen to White Women Cry,'" *Washington Post*, September 11, 2019, https://www.washingtonpost.com

/news/magazine/wp/2019/09/11/feature/how-activist-rachel-cargle-built-a
-business-by-calling-out-racial-injustices-within-feminism.

40. For more information about these organizations and to get
involved, go to https://www.edliberation.org and https://abolitionistteach
ingnetwork.org.

41. Jean Anyon, *Radical Possibilities: Public Policy, Urban Education,
and a New Social Movement* (New York: Routledge, 2014).

42. Robin D. G. Kelley, *Freedom Dreams: The Black Radical Imagination*
(Boston: Beacon Press, 2002), 7.

CHAPTER 1: CURRICULAR TOOLS OF WHITENESS

1. Bree Picower, *Practice What You Teach: Social Justice Education
in the Classroom and the Streets* (New York: Routledge, 2012).

2. John B. King, Amy Mcintosh, and Jennifer Bell-Ellwanger, *The State
of Racial Diversity in the Educator Workforce* (Washington, DC: US Department of Education, Office of Planning, Evaluation and Policy Development, 2016), http://www2.ed.gov/rschstat/eval/highered/racial-diversity
/state-racial-diversity-workforce.pdf.

3. Bill Bigelow, "Presidents and the Enslaved: Helping Students Find
the Truth," Zinn Education Project, 2009, https://www.zinnedproject.org
/wp-content/uploads/2009/10/presidents_and_slaves.pdf.

4. Jacqueline Aboulafia et al., *Diverse City, White Curriculum:
The Exclusion of People of Color from English Language Arts in NYC Schools*
(New York: NYC Coalition for Educational Justice, January 2020), www
.nyccej.org/wp-content/uploads/2019/12/Diverse-City-White-Curriculum
.pdf.

5. NYU Metropolitan Center for Research on Equity and the Transformation of Schools, *Chronically Absent: The Exclusion of People of Color
from NYC Elementary School Curricula* (New York: NYC Coalition for
Educational Justice, February 2019), http://www.nyccej.org/wp-content
/uploads/2019/02/reportCEJ-Chronically-Absent-FINAL.pdf, p. 5. As part
of their organizing to bring attention to this report, CEJ protested in front
of the local board of education and engaged in a Twitter campaign using
the hashtag #CurriculumSoWhite. "3–K" describes early childhood education for three-year-olds.

6. Aboulafia et al., *Diverse City, White Curriculum.*

7. Megan Hester, "Why Is Public School Curriculum Still Whites
Only?," Metropolitan Center for Research on Equity and the Transformation of Schools, December 11, 2018, https://research.steinhardt.nyu.edu
/site/metroblog/2018/12/11/why-is-public-school-curriculum-still-whites-only.

8. Rudine Sims Bishop, "Mirrors, Windows, and Sliding Glass Doors,"

Perspectives 6, no. 3 (Summer 1990), https://scenicregional.org/wp-content
/uploads/2017/08/Mirrors-Windows-and-Sliding-Glass-Doors.pdf.

9. Bishop, "Mirrors, Windows, and Sliding Glass Doors."

10. After contacting five publishers to obtain copyrights to reprint the
examples of racist curriculum described in this chapter, only McGraw-Hill
provided permission for this one image. However, the additional images
are available to view at breepicower.com.

11. Manny Fernandez and Christine Hauser, "Texas Mother Teaches
Textbook Company a Lesson on Accuracy," *New York Times*, October 5,
2015, https://www.nytimes.com/2015/10/06/us/publisher-promises-revisions
-after-textbook-refers-to-african-slaves-as-workers.html.

12. Fernandez and Hauser, "Texas Mother Teaches Textbook
Company a Lesson on Accuracy."

13. Roni Dean-Burren, Facebook post, October 1, 2015, https://www
.facebook.com/roni.deanburren/videos/10208248919206996/?d=n.

14. Ashifa Kassam, "Canada Children's Book Recalled amid Accusa-
tions of Whitewashing History," *Guardian*, October 4, 2017, https://www
.theguardian.com/world/2017/oct/04/canada-childrens-book-recalled
-whitewashing-history.

15. Canadian Press, "Workbook Accused of Whitewashing First
Nations' History Recalled," *Toronto Sun*, October 3, 2017, https://
torontosun.com/2017/10/03/workbook-accused-of-whitewashing-first
-nations-history-to-be-changed/wcm/4f8dd643-d2e4–4741-bc2d-eadbe
1740ido.

16. Eve Tuck and Rubén A. Gaztambide-Fernández, "Curriculum,
Replacement, and Settler Futurity," *Journal of Curriculum Theorizing* 29,
no. 1 (June 18, 2013): 72, http://journal.jctonline.org/index.php/jct/article
/view/411.

17. Tuck and Gaztambide-Fernández, "Curriculum, Replacement,
and Settler Futurity," 74.

18. Laura Whooley, "Last Friday, my 4th graders were studying for our
social studies test and came across text that we felt was inaccurate. . . .,"
Facebook photo post, November 26, 2019, https://www.facebook.com
/photo.php?fbid=10100895530152367&set=pcb.10100895530551567&type
=3&theater.

19. Jenifer Frank, "Lies My Bookshelf Told Me: Slavery in Children's
Literature," *Teaching Tolerance* 62 (Summer 2019), https://www.tolerance
.org/magazine/summer-2019/lies-my-bookshelf-told-me-slavery-in-child
rens-literature.

20. Mary Bowerman, "Scholastic Pulls Controversial George Washington Slave Book," *USA Today*, January 18, 2016, https://www.usatoday.com

/story/money/nation-now/2016/01/18/scholastic-george-washington-slavery
-book/78956160.

21. Eileen Curtright, "My daughter's history text book explains that
saying 'slavery was bad' is too simplistic & many slaves were probably fine
with it," Twitter photo, April 16, 2018, https://twitter.com/eileencurtright
/status/986056826604138497.

22. John H. Bickford III and Cynthia W. Rich, "Examining the Representation of Slavery Within Children's Literature," Social Studies Research
and Practice 9, no. 1 (Spring 2014): 66, http://www.socstrpr.org/wp-content
/uploads/2014/04/MS-06544-Bickford.pdf.

23. Bickford and Rich, "Examining the Representation of Slavery
Within Children's Literature."

24. Hasan Kwame Jeffries, "The Courage to Teach Hard History,"
Teaching Tolerance, February 1, 2018, https://www.tolerance.org/magazine
/the-courage-to-teach-hard-history.

25. Melinda D. Anderson, "Why the Myth of Meritocracy Hurts Kids
of Color," Atlantic, July 27, 2017, https://www.theatlantic.com/education
/archive/2017/07/internalizing-the-myth-of-meritocracy/535035/.

26. David Boddiger, "Texas Charter School Apologizes for Quizzing
Students on 'Positive Aspects' of Slavery," Splinter, April 21, 2018, https://
splinternews.com/texas-charter-school-apologizes-for-quizzing-students
-0-1825446212.

27. Nadia Judith Enchassi, "Homework Assignment Asks Students
to List Positive Aspects of Slavery," KFOR, April 23, 2018, https://kfor.com
/2018/04/23/homework-assignment-asks-students-to-list-positive-aspects
-of-slavery.

28. Associated Press, "'Give 3 Good Reasons for Slavery': Wisconsin
School Apologizes for Slavery Homework Assignment," KDVR, January
11, 2018, https://kdvr.com/2018/01/11/give-3-good-reasons-for-slavery
-wisconsin-school-apologizes-for-slavery-homework-assignment.

29. Trameka Brown-Berry, "Does anyone else find my 4th grader's
homework offensive?," Facebook photo, January 8, 2018, https://www
.facebook.com/photo.php?fbid=10105094231351598&set=a.10101629687
669908&type=3&theater.

30. Enchassi, "Homework Assignment Asks Students to List Positive
Aspects of Slavery."

31. Aaron Blake, "Trump Tries to Re-Write His Own History on
Charlottesville and 'Both Sides,'" Washington Post, April 26, 2019, https://
www.washingtonpost.com/politics/2019/04/25/meet-trump-charlottesville
-truthers.

32. Bill Bigelow and Bob Peterson, Rethinking Columbus: The Next
500 Years (Milwaukee: Rethinking Schools, 1998).

33. Associated Press, "'Give 3 Good Reasons for Slavery.'"

34. Hierospace, "Morrison White Gaze," October 5, 2016, https://www.youtube.com/watch?v=SHHHL3ibFPA.

35. Stan Grant, "Black Writers Courageously Staring Down the White Gaze—This Is Why We All Must Read Them," *Guardian*, December 30, 2015, https://www.theguardian.com/commentisfree/2015/dec/31/black-writers-courageously-staring-down-the-white-gaze-this-is-why-we-all-must-read-them.

36. Eric Wilkinson, "Mom Calls Edmonds School Assignment Racist," K5 News, March 5, 2018, https://www.king5.com/article/news/local/its-just-unbelievable-mom-calls-writing-assignment-racist/281-526038356.

37. Danny Wicentowski, "Missouri School Investigating 'Slave Trade' Homework Assignment," *Riverfront Times*, December 9, 2019, https://www.riverfronttimes.com/newsblog/2019/12/09/missouri-school-investigating-slave-trade-homework-assignment.

38. Wilkinson, "Mom Calls Edmonds School Assignment Racist."

39. Michelle Lou and Brandon Griggs, "State Test Required 10th Graders to Write from a Racist Point of View," CNN, April 4, 2019, https://www.cnn.com/2019/04/04/us/massachusetts-test-racist-underground-railroad-trnd/index.html.

40. Lou and Griggs, "State Test Required 10th Graders to Write from a Racist Point of View."

41. "Educators' Unions and Civil Rights Groups Demand That DESE Withdraw Racially Offensive MCAS," Massachusetts Teachers Association, April 3, 2019, https://massteacher.org/news/2019/04/unions-and-civil-rights-groups-demand-that-dese-withdraw-racially-offensive-mcas.

42. Ravi Baichwal, "Naperville Central High School Student Charged with Hate Crime after Allegedly Posting Racist Craigslist Ad," ABC7 Chicago, November 20, 2019, https://abc7chicago.com/naperville-student-charged-with-hate-crime-after-allegedly-posting-racist-craigslist-ad/5709478.

43. Vikram Dodd, "Children Whitening Skin to Avoid Racial Hate Crime, Charity Finds," *Guardian*, May 29, 2019, https://www.theguardian.com/society/2019/may/30/children-whitening-skin-to-avoid-racial-hate-charity-finds.

44. Bethania Palma Markus, "'Kenyans Are Able to Run Very Fast': Publisher Blasted for Kids' Books Full of Racial Stereotypes," *Raw Story*, September 10, 2015, https://www.rawstory.com/2015/09/kenyans-are-able-to-run-very-fast-publisher-blasted-for-kids-books-full-of-racial-stereotypes.

45. Markus, "'Kenyans Are Able to Run Very Fast.'"

46. Monique Judge, "I have a rant incoming about racism and the

messages that are sent to our children on the low in their schools. (Thread)," Twitter posts, February 14, 2017, https://twitter.com/the journalista/status/831723476524294145?ref_src=twsrc%5Etfw%7Ctwcamp %5Etweetembed%7Ctwterm%5E831723476524294145&ref_url=http%3 A%2F%2Fmic.com%2Farticles%2F168666%2Ffor-black-history-month -black-second-graders-at-la-school-receive-math-.

47. Jorge Rivas, "Atlanta School Sends 8-Year Olds with Math Home-work About Beating Slaves," *Colorlines*, January 10, 2012, https://www .colorlines.com/articles/atlanta-school-sends-8-year-olds-math-homework -about-beating-slaves.

48. Lia Eustachewich, Joe Tacopino, and Yoav Gonen, "Midtown Teacher Includes Questions About Slavery in Elementary School Math Homework," *New York Post*, February 22, 2013, https://nypost.com/2013 /02/22/midtown-teacher-includes-questions-about-slavery-in-elementary -school-math-homework.

49. Bult, "Alabama Middle School Causes Outrage for Handing Out Math Quiz with Blatant Gang References."

50. Marc Torrence, "See Controversial Math Quiz That Got Alabama Teacher Put on Leave," Patch Across America, June 2, 2016, https://patch .com/us/across-america/see-8th-grade-math-quiz-got-alabama-teacher-put -leave-0. Stephen A. Crockett Jr., "Ala. Teacher Gives Test to 8th-Graders Asking How Many Tricks Would a 'Ho' Have to Turn to Support Pimp's Crack Habit," *Root*, June 1, 2016, https://www.theroot.com/ala-teacher -gives-test-to-8th-graders-asking-how-many-1790855483.

51. Bult, "Alabama Middle School Causes Outrage for Handing Out Math Quiz with Blatant Gang References."

52. Julius Davis and Christopher C. Jett, *Critical Race Theory in Mathematics Education* (New York: Routledge, 2019).

53. Andrew Scott Baron and Mahzarin R. Banaji, "The Development of Implicit Attitudes: Evidence of Race Evaluations from Ages 6 and 10 and Adulthood," *Psychological Science* 17, no. 1 (January 2006): 53, https:// doi.org/10.1111/j.1467-9280.2005.01664.x.

54. Jean Anyon, "Social Class and the Hidden Curriculum of Work," *Journal of Education* 162, no. 1 (Winter 1980): 67–92, www.jstor/org/stable /42741976.

55. Annie Reneau, "This Kids' Worksheet Is a Perfect Example of How Implicit Bias Gets Perpetuated," Our Three Winners, January 16, 2019, https://ourthreewinners.org/this-kids-worksheet-is-a-perfect-example-of -how-implicit-bias-gets-perpetuated.

56. Aqkhira S-Aungkh, Facebook post, January 3, 2019, https://www .facebook.com/photo.php?fbid=10155648000740356&set=a.55411285355& type=3&theater.

57. Reneau, "This Kids' Worksheet Is a Perfect Example of How Implicit Bias Gets Perpetuated."

58. Peter Holley, "'Super Racist' Pool Safety Poster Prompts Red Cross Apology," *Washington Post*, June 27, 2016, https://www.washingtonpost.com /news/morning-mix/wp/2016/06/27/super-racist-pool-safety-poster-prompts -red-cross-apology.

59. Holley, "'Super Racist' Pool Safety Poster Prompts Red Cross Apology."

60. Ellen Moynihan and Ben Chapman, "Mock Student Slave Auction Rocks Private Westchester School," *New York Daily News*, March 8, 2019, https://www.nydailynews.com/new-york/education/ny-metro-mock-slave -auction-riles-westchester-school-20190308-story.html.

61. Headlines may be found at the following sites: https://13wham.com /news/local/watertown-teacher-accused-of-making-black-students-act-as -slaves-in-mock-auction; https://www.complex.com/life/2019/03/teacher -white-students-bid-black-classmates-mock-slave-auction; https://www.the root.com/wisconsin-teacher-reportedly-asks-7th-graders-to-create-18340038 78; https://www.wect.com/2019/03/09/monopoly-like-slavery-game-played -by-fourth-grade-nc-class-outrages-african-american-grandmother/; https:// www.loudountimes.com/news/for-black-history-month-this-loudoun-county -elementary-school-played-a-runaway-slave-game-in/article_9cecd568-35ef -11e9-8540-6372d03d3025.html; https://www.usatoday.com/story/news/edu cation/2019/09/10/western-middle-school-indiana-cancels-slave-ship-role -play-lesson/2276633001/; https://www.amren.com/news/2019/02/south -carolina-mom-outraged-after-kids-told-to-pick-cotton-sing-slave-song -as-game.

62. Anderson, *White Rage*.

63. Joshua Espinoza, "Elementary Teacher Placed on Leave After Allegedly Holding Mock Slave Auction," *Complex*, May 31, 2019, https:// www.complex.com/life/2019/05/elementary-teacher-on-leave-holding -mock-slave-auction.

64. Matthew Grant, "South Carolina Mom Outraged After Kids Told to Pick Cotton, Sing Slave Song as 'Game,'" FOX 46 Charlotte, February 26, 2019, www.fox46.com/news/south-carolina-mom-outraged-after-kids -told-to-pick-cotton-sing-slave-song-as-game.

65. Southern Poverty Law Center, *Teaching the Hard History of American Slavery* (2018), https://www.splcenter.org/teaching-hard-history -american-slavery; Melinda D. Anderson, "What Kids Are Really Learning About Slavery," *Atlantic*, February 1, 2018, https://www.theatlantic.com /education/archive/2018/02/what-kids-are-really-learning-about-slavery /552098; P. R. Lockhart, "American Schools Can't Figure Out How to Teach Kids About Slavery," *Vox*, May 30, 2019, https://www.vox.com

/identities/2019/3/13/18262240/mock-slave-auction-new-york-school-teacher
-investigation.

66. Erhabor Ighodaro, "Curriculum Violence: The New Civil Rights
Issue—How Efforts at Standardization Impact the Academic Achievement
of African Americans," in *Still Not Equal: Expanding Educational Opportunity in Society*, ed. M Christopher Brown II (New York: Peter Lang, 2007),
229–38.

67. James W. Loewen, *Lies My Teacher Told Me: Everything Your Ameri-
can History Textbook Got Wrong* (New York: New Press, 2008); Howard
Zinn, *A People's History of the United States: 1492–Present* (New York:
Harper Perennial, 2003).

68. Carter Godwin Woodson, *The Mis-Education of the Negro*
(Washington, DC: Associated Publishers, 1933), 24.

69. Rob Nixon, *Slow Violence and the Environmentalism of the Poor*
(Cambridge, MA: Harvard University Press, 2011).

70. Nixon, *Slow Violence and the Environmentalism of the Poor*, 2.

71. Maria Trent et al., "The Impact of Racism on Child and Adolescent Health," *Pediatrics* 144, no. 2 (August 1, 2019), https://doi.org/10.1542
/peds.2019-1765.

72. Vincent J. Felitti et al., "Relationship of Childhood Abuse and
Household Dysfunction to Many of the Leading Causes of Death in
Adults: The Adverse Childhood Experiences (ACEs) Study," *American
Journal of Preventative Medicine* 14, no. 4 (May 1, 1998), https://doi
.org/10.1016/S0749-3797(98)00017-8.

73. Vanessa Sacks and David Murphey, "The Prevalence of Adverse
Childhood Experiences, Nationally, by State, and by Race or Ethnicity,"
Child Trends, February 20, 2018, https://www.childtrends.org/publications
/prevalence-adverse-childhood-experiences-nationally-state-race-ethnicity.

74. Angela Helm, "Pediatricians: Black Children Suffer Significantly
from Racism," *Root*, August 9, 2019, https://www.theroot.com/pediatricians
-black-children-suffer-significantly-from-1837105296.

75. Sacks and Murphey, "The Prevalence of Adverse Childhood
Experiences, Nationally, by State, and by Race or Ethnicity."

76. Sacks and Murphey, "The Prevalence of Adverse Childhood
Experiences, Nationally, by State, and by Race or Ethnicity."

77. Melissa Merrick et al., "Prevalence of Adverse Childhood Experiences from the 2011–2014 Behavioral Risk Factor Surveillance System in
23 States," *JAMA Pediatrics* 172, no. 11 (September 17, 2018): 1038–44,
https://doi.org/10.1001/jamapediatrics.2018.2537.

78. Carrie Gaffney, "When Schools Cause Trauma," *Teaching Tolerance*
62 (Summer 2019), https://www.tolerance.org/magazine/summer-2019
/when-schools-cause-trauma.

79. Trent et al., "The Impact of Racism on Child and Adolescent Health."

80. Emily Alford, "Long Island Teacher Reportedly Asked Students to Provide Funny Captions for Images of Slavery," *Jezebel*, September 27, 2019, https://jezebel.com/long-island-teacher-reportedly-asked-students-to -provid-1838508745.

CHAPTER 2: THE ICEBERG

1. Paul P. Murphy, "White Nationalists Use Tiki Torches to Light Up Charlottesville March," CNN, August 14, 2017, https://www.cnn .com/2017/08/12/us/white-nationalists-tiki-torch-march-trnd/index.html.

2. In *Racism Without Racists*, author Eduardo Bonilla-Silva described the process of avoiding the recognition of race as "color-blind," yet critical disability scholars have complicated the term, critiquing the way it "likens a lack of vision to ignorance" (Subini Ancy Annamma, David Connor, and Beth Ferri, "Dis/Ability Critical Race Studies (DisCrit): Theorizing at the Intersections of Race and Dis/Ability," *Race Ethnicity and Education* 16, no. 1 [2013]: 1–31), and recommend a shift to Ruth Frankenberg's (*White Women, Race Matters: The Social Construction of Whiteness*, [Minneapolis: University of Minnesota Press, 1993]) and Anna Stubblefield's (*Ethics Along the Color Line* [Ithaca, NY: Cornell University Press, 2005]) use of the term "color-evasive," which "refuses to position people who are blind as embodying deficit" (Annamma et al., 6). In a past coedited book, *Confronting Racism in Teacher Education: Counternarratives of Critical Practice* (New York: Routledge, 2017), Rita Kohli and I began using the term "race-evasive" because we found meaning in Bonilla-Silva's definition of the concept and in Annamma et al.'s critique, but additionally wanted to avoid the use of "color" as a proxy for "race."

3. Joel H. Spring, *Deculturalization and the Struggle for Equality: A Brief History of the Education of Dominated Cultures in the United States*, 7th ed. (New York: McGraw-Hill, 2013).

4. Antonio Gramsci, *Prison Notebooks*, Vol. 2 (New York: Columbia University Press, 1992).

5. Tatum, *Why Are All the Black Kids Sitting Together in the Cafeteria?*

CHAPTER 3: REFRAMING UNDERSTANDINGS OF RACE WITHIN TEACHER EDUCATION

1. Arianna MacNeill, "A Boy Was Sent to the Principal's Office. Then an Administrator Used the N-Word," Boston.com, October 8, 2019, https://www.boston.com/news/local-news/2019/10/08/maine-student-racial -slur-incident.

2. Sarah Jackson, "Pennsylvania Teacher Placed on Leave for Racist

Rant to Parent after Fender Bender," NBC News, October 11, 2019, https://
www.nbcnews.com/news/us-news/pennsylvania-teacher-placed-leave-racist
-rant-parent-after-fender-bender-n1065121.

3. Eli Rosenberg, "Idaho Teachers Dress as 'Mexicans' and Trump's
MAGA Wall for Halloween," *Washington Post*, November 5, 2018,
https://www.washingtonpost.com/nation/2018/11/03/these-school-teachers
-dressed-up-mexicans-wall-halloween-it-didnt-go-well/.

4. Elise Solé, " 'Trump Can Deport You': Teacher Terminated for
Threatening Boy Who Didn't Say, 'Yes, Sir,' " Yahoo! Life, August 30, 2019,
https://www.yahoo.com/lifestyle/trump-can-deport-you-teacher-terminated
-for-threatening-boy-who-didnt-say-yes-sir-210141857.html.

5. Ben Chapman, Andy Mai, and Stephen Rex Brown, "Blackface
Photos Used in Brooklyn PTA Fund-Raiser Message Ignite Outrage,"
New York Daily News, February 12, 2018, https://www.nydailynews.com
/new-york/education/blackface-photos-pta-fund-raiser-message-ignite
-outrage-article-1.3814759; Kia Morgan-Smith, "Teacher Fired after Telling
Elementary School Student, 'You're Lucky I'm Not Making You Pick Cotton,' " *Grio*, June 13, 2019, https://thegrio.com/2019/06/13/teacher-fired
-after-telling-elementary-school-student-youre-lucky-im-not-making-you
-pick-cotton.

6. AJ Willingham, "Middle School Teacher Secretly Ran White
Supremacist Podcast, Says It Was Satire," CNN, March 6, 2018, https://
www.cnn.com/2018/03/05/us/dayanna-volitich-white-nationalist-florida
-school-podcast-trnd/index.html; Ibn Safir, "Teachers Pose With Noose,
Earn Suspensions Alongside Principal," *Root*, May 11, 2019, https://www
.theroot.com/picture-of-smiling-teachers-holding-noose-lands-all-fou-1834
694657; Montana Couser, "Teacher Who Made a Noose Symbol Toward
Black Kid Won't Face Charges; DA's Office Said It Wasn't a Hate Crime,"
Root, July 25, 2018, https://www.theroot.com/teacher-who-made-a-noose
-symbol-toward-black-kid-doesnt-1827870718?fbclid=IwAR1NMojNYei
73XcvT_6gEQLqLeXN_DFEM2kmwYOLkoftL1aOpWyJfgs7MJE.

7. "Prosecutor Admits It Was Wrong to Charge a Child Playing
Dodgeball," NewsOne, August 9, 2019, https://newsone.com/3883947
/prosecutor-admits-wrong-dodgeball-kym-worthy; Luke Darby, "Florida
Police Officer Arrested and Handcuffed a 6-Year-Old Black Girl for a
Tantrum in Class," GQ, September 23, 2019, https://www.gq.com/story
/six-year-old-black-girl-arrested-for-a-tantrum.

8. Michael J. Dumas, " 'Losing an Arm': Schooling as a Site of Black
Suffering," *Race Ethnicity and Education* 17, no. 1 (2014): 1–29, https://doi
.org/10.1080/13613324.2013.850412.

9. Jamila Lyiscott, *Black Appetite. White Food: Issues of Race, Voice,
and Justice Within and Beyond the Classroom* (New York: Routledge, 2019).

10. Kevin K. Kumashiro, *The Seduction of Common Sense: How the Right Has Framed the Debate on America's Schools* (New York: Teachers College Press, 2008), 3; George Lakoff, *Don't Think of an Elephant! Know Your Values and Frame the Debate: The Essential Guide for Progressives* (White River Junction, VT: Chelsea Green Publishing, 2004).

11. Kumashiro, *The Seduction of Common Sense*, 3.

12. Data was collected from eight years of coursework for a yearlong social justice and curriculum design course. The course had several major objectives. It was designed to orient the students to the context of Newark, New Jersey, to support them to teach from a racial justice perspective, to help them develop an assets-based view of the city, and to teach them the foundations of curriculum design. Data included periodic reflection papers ranging from three to five pages, a racial autobiography of five to ten pages in which they reflected on the role that race has played throughout their life, and blog postings in which they reflected on community events they attended. The bulk of the data came from a reflection paper from the two-day Undoing Racism workshop by People's Institute for Survival and Beyond and their course culminating final papers, approximately ten to fifteen pages, in which students were specifically asked to reflect on their journey of the year, new understandings they felt they developed, and which experiences helped to shape this new awareness. I read through the papers for examples of new understandings of race the teachers identified. I wrote codes in margins, creating short line-by-line units, staying as close to the participants' words as possible. After finalizing line-by-line codes, I lifted the codes and corresponding text out of interview transcripts and recategorized them into "focused codes" based on connections across line-by-line codes that represented larger themes. I physically cut these line-by-line units, with only a color-coded system as to who said what, creating piles of data that shared similar themes. These piles were checked for consistency and put into envelopes, each titled with a label that described the phenomenon within. As I arranged these labels and thought about the relationship among them, my conceptual framework emerged as the story these labels told together.

13. Loewen, *Lies My Teacher Told Me*.

14. Anderson, *White Rage*.

15. To learn more about how racial categories were created by scientists to justify colonization and slavery, I recommend Ibram X. Kendi's two books, *Stamped from the Beginning: The Definitive History of Racist Ideas in America* and *How to Be an Antiracist*. *Stamped from the Beginning* has also been adapted with Jason Reynolds into a young adult edition. The PBS series *Race: The Power of an Illusion* illustrates how various legal rulings create and change racial categories, refuting biological arguments of racial difference. I highly recommend attending the two-day workshop Undoing

Racism, put on by the People's Institute for Survival and Beyond. Their website includes an event calendar: www.pisb.org.

16. The People's Institute for Survival and Beyond, "Undoing Racism," workshop, https://www.pisab.org/programs, accessed January 9, 2020.

17. Ibram X. Kendi, *How to Be an Antiracist* (New York: One World, 2019), 41.

18. Coined by Clance and Imes (P. R. Clance and S. A. Imes, "The Imposter Phenomenon in High Achieving Women: Dynamics and Therapeutic Intervention," *Psychotherapy: Theory, Research & Practice* 15. no. 3 [1978]: 241–47, https://doi.org/10.1037/h0086006), *imposter phenomenon* refers to internalized feeling that individuals, often from marginalized identities, hold that they did not earn their accomplishments and do not deserve success or belonging. First identified in research on women, the phenomenon is now used to describe the ways in which racism is internalized by high-achieving people of Color. Pauline Rose Clance and Maureen Ann O'Toole, "The Imposter Phenomenon," *Women & Therapy* 6, no. 3 (December 16, 1987): 51–64, https://doi.org/10.1300/J015V06N03_05; Gregory M. Walton and Geoffrey L. Cohen, "A Question of Belonging: Race, Social Fit, and Achievement," *Journal of Personality and Social Psychology* 92, no. 1 (January 2007): 82–96, https://doi.org/10.1037/0022-3514.92.1.82.

19. Dismantling Racism Works, "Internalizations," *Dismantling Racism Works Web Workbook,* http://www.dismantlingracism.org/internalizations .html, accessed February 15, 2020.

20. Derman-Sparks and Phillips, *Teaching/Learning Anti-Racism.*

21. Pedro Noguera, *City Schools and the American Dream: Reclaiming the Promise of Public Education* (New York: Teachers College Press, 2003).

22. Noguera, *City Schools and the American Dream.*

23. Gloria Ladson-Billings, "From the Achievement Gap to the Education Debt: Understanding Achievement in US Schools," *Educational Researcher* 35, no. 7 (October 2006): 3–12, https://doi.org/10.3102/0013189 X035007003; Theresa Perry, Claude Steele, and Asa G. Hilliard, *Young, Gifted, and Black: Promoting High Achievement Among African-American Students* (Boston: Beacon Press, 2003).

24. Rochelle Gutierrez explains the very helpful use of this term: "I use the term 'historically looted' instead of 'low income' to highlight the ongoing domination these students face and the benefits dominant members of society reap as a result." See https://www.todos-math.org/assets/documents /TEEM/teem7_final1.pdf.

CHAPTER 4: DISRUPTING WHITENESS IN TEACHER EDUCATION

1. *Respectability politics* refers to the concept that members of an oppressed group must adopt the norms and behaviors of the dominant

group in order to achieve mainstream success. Members of the oppressed groups uphold respectability politics by judging and shaming group members who do not assimilate and blame those individuals, rather than a system of oppression, for lack of advancement along the social ladder.

2. Picower and Kohli, *Confronting Racism in Teacher Education*; Gabriella Gutiérrez y Muhs et al., eds., *Presumed Incompetent: The Intersections of Race and Class for Women in Academia* (Louisville: University Press of Colorado, 2012).

3. For a detailed explanation of Four I's, see page 10.

4. For more information on restorative circles, see Carolyn Boyes-Watson and Kay Pranis, *Circle Forward: Building a Restorative School Community* (St. Paul, MN: Living Justice Press, 2015).

5. To read more about patterns of how White women enact racial power, see Luvvie Ajayi's blog post in which she differentiates various manifestations of Whiteness. Luvvie Ajayi, "About Caucasity and the Difference Between a Becky, a Karen and a Susan," *Awesomely Luvvie*, 2020, https://www.awesomelyluvvie.com/2020/04/caucasity-karen-becky -susan.html.

CHAPTER 5: HUMANIZING RACIAL JUSTICE IN TEACHER EDUCATION

1. Rita Kohli et al., "Critical Professional Development: Centering the Social Justice Needs of Teachers," *International Journal of Critical Pedagogy* 6, no. 2 (2015).

2. Bree Picower, "Can We Get You There from Here? Political Clarity in the Teacher Education Admissions Process by Dr. Bree Picower," Equity Alliance, 2019, http://www.niusileadscape.org/bl/can-we-get-you-there -from-here-political-clarity-in-the-teacher-education-admissions-process -by-dr-bree-picower.

3. This program was excluded from the findings because this chapter is examining teacher education programs that work to mitigate White teachers from enacting harm. I therefore focused on programs that have White students.

4. Picower, "Can We Get You There from Here?"

5. Rosa L. Rivera-McCutchen, "'We Don't Got Time for Grumbling': Toward an Ethic of Radical Care in Urban School Leadership," *Educational Administration Quarterly* (May 2020), https://doi:10.1177/0013161 X20925892.

6. Marisa Meltzer, "'I Refuse to Listen to White Women Cry,'" *Washington Post Magazine*, September 11, 2019, https://www.washingtonpost .com/news/magazine/wp/2019/09/11/feature/how-activist-rachel-cargle -built-a-business-by-calling-out-racial-injustices-within-feminism.

7. April Dawn Harter/Racism Recovery Center, "I Was Wrong to Tell

You to De-Center Your Feelings, White People," *Medium*, 2019, https://medium.com/@racismrecoverycenter/i-was-wrong-to-tell-you-to-de-center-your-feelings-white-people-65a7948f383d.

8. Shawn Ginwright, *Hope and Healing in Urban Education: How Urban Activists and Teachers Are Reclaiming Matters of the Heart* (New York: Routledge, 2015).

9. Django Paris and H. Samy Alim, "What Are We Seeking to Sustain Through Culturally Sustaining Pedagogy? A Loving Critique Forward," *Harvard Educational Review* 84, no. 1 (April 2014): 85–100, https://doi.org/10.17763/haer.84.1.982l873k2ht16m77.

INDEX

Figures and notes are indicated by "f" and "n" following the page number.

AAP (American Academy of Pediatrics), 58–59
Abolitionist Teaching Network, 20
accreditation, RJPs and, 140
achievement gap, source of, 100–1
admissions, for RJPs, 114–15, 144–47
Adverse Childhood Experiences (ACE) score, 59
All Things Being Equal tool, 39–43
allyship, nature of, 17
American Academy of Pediatrics (AAP), 58–59
American Dream, ideology of, 12
American meritocracy, idea of, 66–67
American Red Cross, safe swimming campaign poster, 53–54
Anderson, Carol, 56
anti-Blackness, 10, 158
anti-racism, 15–16, 98
Anyon, Jean, 23
archeology of the self, 13
Atlantic slave trade, textbook example of, 30–32, 31f

authentic emotions, strategies of Whiteness versus, 149–52
Ayers, Bill, 119

Baldwin, James, 83
beliefs: influences on teaching, 108; institutional racism as manifestation of teachers' beliefs, 99
biases, internalized biases, 97 98
Bickford, John H., 37–38
Bigelow, Bill, 27–28
BIPOC (Black, Indigenous, and people of Color): in colleges of education, 111; erasure of, 27–30; institutional racism and, 98; Not That Bad tool and, 35; students, as targets of racism, 38; use of term, 10; White attitudes toward, 67; White Gaze tool and, 47, 48. *See also* children of Color; students of Color (in RJPs)
A Birthday Cake for George Washington (Ganeshram), 35–36, 37
Bishop, Rudine Sims, 29–30

Black Appetite, White Food
(Lyiscott), 86
Black Lives Matter (BLM) move-
ment, 16
Black people, racism against, 10.
See also anti-Blackness; BIPOC
blame, 30–36, 31*f*, 91, 100–2
Blumenbach, Johann Friedrich, 90
Bonds, Anne, 10
Bonilla-Silva, Eduardo, 187n2
Bridges, Ruby, 67–68
Brown-Berry, Trameka, 40, 43
Burns Middle School (Alabama),
13–14, 51–52
Burren, Coby, 30
Burson, Esther, 39

calling-in, 124
call-out (cancel) culture, 124
Camangian, Patrick "Cam": on
admissions to RJPs, 146; on
student-teacher relationships,
148; on Whiteness, emergence
in classes, 119, 123–24
Cara (teacher), 73–75
Cargle, Rachel, 150
Carson Dellosa (publisher), 52
case studies: openmindedness
case study, 70–73; overview of,
64–65; questioning case study,
73–75; transformation case
study, 75–81; White protectionism case study, 65–70
CEJ (Coalition for Educational
Justice), 28–29, 180n5
Center for Racial Justice in Education (CRJE), 85, 91
centering race, foreshadowing
the experience of, 115–17
Center X (UCLA), 138–39, 141,
163
charity, movement to justice
from, 102–3

chattel slavery, 32–39, 44–47,
50–51, 54–57
children: Adverse Childhood
Experiences (ACE) scores,
59–60; response to racial hate
crimes, 48–49; White children,
White Gaze tool and, 47–48
children of Color: RJPs' accountability to, 131–32; traumatization of, 47, 55, 57, 58–60
children's books, 29–30, 71–72
classes, disruption of Whiteness
in, 109–12, 118–24
Coalition for Educational Justice
(CEJ), 28–29, 180n5
co-conspirators, Whites as, 17,
124, 166
cohorts, organization of RJP students into, 155–57
collaboration, importance of, 80
colleges of education, description
of, 111
color-blind, as term, critiques of,
187n2
color-evasive, as term, 187n2
Columbus, Christopher, 42–43, 88
community and community
engagement, 80, 161–63
Cortland's Urban Recruitment
of Educators (CURE, SUNY
Cortland), 144
counseling students out, creation
of structures for, 129–31
coursework in RJPs, explicitness
about race in, 117–18
critical professional development
(CPD), 141–42
CRJE (Center for Racial Justice
in Education), 85, 91
culture: racial identity versus,
94–96; White cultural norms
in schools, questioning of,
106–7

CURE (Cortland's Urban Recruitment of Educators, SUNY Cortland), 144
current inequalities, historical racism as shaping, 87–89
curricular Tools of Whiteness, 25–62; All Things Being Equal tool, 39–43; #CurriculumSoWhite response cycle, 60–62, 61f; curriculum violence, 57–58; Dawn's use of, 66–69; educational malpractice, 58–60; Embedded Stereotypes tool, 49–54; introduction to, 21, 25–27; justifications for, 93; No One Is to Blame tool, 30–36, 31f; Not That Bad tool, 36–39; Racist Reproduction tool, 54–57; RJPs and, 114; White Gaze tool, 43–49; White Out tool, 27–30
curriculum, basis in ideology, 13
#CurriculumSoWhite, 1–24; introduction to, 1–2; levels of oppression and advantage in, 11–12; oppression, four levels of, 10–12; Picower, as White scholar writing about race, 14–21; proliferation, reasons for, 167; response cycle, 60–62, 61f; stress reactions to, 60; teacher education, as space for transformation of racial ideology, 13–14; use as hashtag, 2; viral racist curriculum, 2–5; White socialization, 5–10
curriculum violence, 57–58
Curtright, Eileen, 37, 181–2n18
Cushing, Bonnie, 95–96

Davis, Julius, 52
Dawn (first-grade teacher), 12, 65–70, 94
Dayes, Nicole, 56–57
Dean-Burren, Roni, 30–31
default settings, shift to anti-racism, 81–82
Diana (teacher), 63, 76–81, 105–6
DiAngelo, Robin, 18, 20, 118
diary writing exercise, 44–46
discomfort, in discussions of race, 116
Dismantling Racism (Jones and Okun), 8
Dismantling Racism: 2016 Workbook (Ayvazian et al.), 178n19
Dismantling Racism Works Web Workbook (dRworks), 93
Diverse City, White Curriculum (CEJ), 28–29
diversity: lack of, in toys, 77–78; multiple perspectives in, 72
Du Bois, W. E. B., 1, 3

education: educational malpractice, 58–60; education debt, 101; functions of, 21. See also entries beginning "teacher education"
Education for Liberation Network, 20, 166
Embedded Stereotypes tool, 49–54
emotions, 124, 138, 147–53
enslavement: All Things Being Equal tool and, 40; construction of racism and, 87; curricular tools of Whiteness and, 25; Embedded Stereotype tool and, 50–51; mentioned, 21; No One Is to Blame tool and, 30–39, 31f; Racist Reproduction tool and, 54–57; White Gaze tool and, 44–47
environmental racism, 74–75
erasures: of BIPOC, 27–30

A *Fine Dessert* (Jenkins), 35, 36
First Nations people, No One Is to Blame tool and, 32.
    See also Indigenous people
Flourish Agenda, 154
Four I's of oppression and advantage, 10–12, 62, 85–87, 155, 158, 163, 167
Fox News, 39
frames, description of, 86
Francois, Annamarie: on accreditation and RJPs, 140; on cohorts, 156; on community engagement, 163; on counseling students out of RJPs, 132; on finding teacher mentors, 141; on foreshadowing race-centered discussions, 115–16; on hiring, 138–39; on induction support, 164–65; on internal racial justice work, 143–44; on recruiting for RJPs, 145; on relationships in RJPs, 148
Freedom Dreams, 23
Fugitive Literacies Framework, 86
Fujiyoshi, Kay: on cohorts, 156; on community engagement, 162; on counseling students out of RJPs, 130–31; on induction period, 164; on one-on-one meetings with students, 19, 152; on race, centering of, 118; on student recruiting for RJPs, 146–47; on students, relationships with, 153; on sweet poison versus bitter medicine, 135; UTEP program, changes to, 113; on Whiteness, disruption of, 119; on White students' emotions, 151

Gallagher, Blaine, 44, 47
Ganeshram, Ramin, 35–36

Garza, Alicia, 16
gaze, White Gaze tool, 43–49
Gaztambide-Fernández, Rubén A., 32–33
GI Bill, 88
Ginwright, Shawn, 154–55
Godfrey, Erin B., 38–39
going viral, pattern of, 3
Grace (teacher), 70–73
The Guardian (newspaper), on children's response to racial hate crimes, 48–49
Gutierrez, Rochelle, 190n24

Hall, Stuart, 5–6
harm, done by teachers. *See* curricular Tools of Whiteness
Hart, Ericka, 17
Harter, April Dawn, 153
Hay, Louise, 25
health, slow violence's impact on, 58–60
hegemony, 78–79
Hester, Megan, 29
Heyer, Heather, 41
Hilliard, Asa, 101
historically looted communities, 103, 161, 190n24
historical racism, 3, 87–89
hostile racial climate, 84, 111
Howard, Gary, 67, 156
Howard, Tyrone: on addressing student resistance, 119–20; on collective engagement with internal work of racial justice, 143; mentioned, 123; on Whiteness as part of the RJP curriculum, 120–21, 122

identity, cognizance of, when teaching about race, 105–6
identity caucusing (racial affinity spaces), 157–58

ideology: definition of, 5–6; ideological racial advantage, 11; ideological racial reframes, 87–91. *See also* racial ideology and curriculum
Ighodaro, Erhabor, 57–58
Imani, Blair, 38
implicit bias, 52–53
imposter syndrome, 91, 190n18
Indigenous people (Native Americans): Columbus Day and, 88; crimes against, 6; lack of fear of potential backlash from, 43; No One Is to Blame tool and, 32–33; readings on, personal change and, 77; as targets of racial curriculum, 10; White Gaze tool and, 44–47
induction period, 164
institutions: institutional racial advantage, 11; institutional racial reframes, 98–103; institutional racism, as manifestation of teachers' beliefs, 99
internalized racial oppression and advantage, 11, 26, 33, 47, 48–49
internalized racial reframes, 92–98
interpersonal/individual racial oppression, 11
interpersonal racial reframes, 103–7
Inwood, Joshua, 10

Jeffries, Hasan Kwame, 38
Jenkins, Emily, 35, 36
Jensen, Robert, 6
Jerome (fourth-grader), 41
Jett, Christopher C., 52
Johnson, Tre, 18
Jones, Kenneth, 8
Judge, Monique, 183n46

justice, movement from charity to, 102–3

"Karens," 126–27
Kelley, Robin D. G., 23
Kendi, Ibram X., 9, 189n15
Kennedy, Bill: on induction support, 164–65; mentioned, 112; on one-on-one meetings with students, 159–60; on relationships in RJPs, 149; on RJP teams, 136; on role as White person, 128; on UTEP, evolution of, 113; on Whiteness, learning opportunities from, 121
Kincheloe, Joe L., 7
Kohli, Rita, 187n2
Kumashiro, Kevin, 86

Ladson-Billings, Gloria, 101
Lakoff, George, 86
Laurel (student), 34–35
lead, in school water supplies, 74–75
Linnaeus, Carl, 90
Little Books series (Reading Horizons), 49–50
Livar, Roberto, 39–40
Love, Bettina, 17, 20, 136
Lyiscott, Jamila, 86

Maloney, Tanya: Four I's, use of, 11; on institutional leadership, support from, 131, 139; mentioned, 114; on Newark Teacher Project, 117; on professional development for teacher mentors, 142; racial affinity groups, work with, 158; on Whiteness, disruption of, 125; on White RJP students as a minority, 156–57

Manú (student), 40–41
Marx, Sherry, 8–9
Massachusetts Comprehensive
    Assessment System (MCAS)
    exam, 47–48
mathematics, Embedded Stereo-
    types tools used in, 50–52
McGraw-Hill, 2, 30, 34
Me and White Supremacy (Saad), 8
mentor teacher, in RJPs, 140–42
Metropolitan Center for Research
    on Equity and the Transfor-
    mation of Schools (New York
    University), 29
Mobile, Alabama, racist math-
    ematics test, 13–14
money, as social construct, 91
Montclair State University, New-
    ark Teacher Project (NTP), 11,
    114, 141–42, 158
Morrison, Toni, 43

National Survey of Children's
    Health (NSCH), 59–60
Native Americans. See Indigenous
    people
Newark, New Jersey, water crisis,
    74
Newark Montclair Urban Teacher
    Residency Program, 137
Newark Teacher Project (NTP,
    Montclair State University),
    11, 114, 141–42, 158
New York University, Metro-
    politan Center for Research on
    Equity and the Transformation
    of Schools, 29
Nixon, Rob, 58
No One Is to Blame tool, 30–36,
    31f
Not That Bad tool, 36–39
NSCH (National Survey of
    Children's Health), 59–60

NTP (Newark Teacher Project,
    Montclair State University),
    11, 114, 141–42, 158

Okun, Tema, 8
omissions, in educational material,
    27–30
one-on-one meetings, 159–61
openmindedness case study, 70–73
opportunity gap, 101
oppression and advantage. See
    Four I's of oppression and
    advantage
Ortiz, Natalia, 91

Paris, Django, 1, 2
PBS, series on racial categories,
    189n15
PD (professional development)
    on racial justice, 141
people of Color. See BIPOC;
    children of Color; students
    of Color (in RJPs)
People's Institute for Survival and
    Beyond, 89, 189n15
Picower, Bree: Jewish background,
    influence of, 94–96; on
    race-evasive as term, 187n2;
    research methodology for
    data collection, 189n12; as
    RJP codirector, 112; White
    fragility of, 118; Whiteness,
    own experiences with, 118; as
    White scholar writing about
    race, 14–21
plantation owner, poster assign-
    ment on, 44, 45–46
post-graduation teacher support,
    163–66
Pour-Khorshid, Farima: on feel-
    ings, 150; on Harter article,
    153; on healing harm, 154–55;
    on internal work of racial

justice, 142–43; on one-on-one meetings with students, 160–61; on race, explicitness about, 117; on racial affinity spaces, 157–58; on student recruiting for RJPs, 146; on UESJ, 154; on unlearning racism, 152; on Whiteness, disruption of, 121

poverty tourism, 161

Prentice Hall, 37

Prescott Elementary (Oakland, California), 14, 15

preservice teachers: racism of, 8–9; recruiting and admitting, into RJPs, 144–47. See also *entries beginning "teacher education"*

presidents, as enslavers, 28

privilege, importance of understanding sources of, 97

professional development (PD) on racial justice, 141

program teams, 136–47; collective engagement in internal work of racial justice, 142–44; hiring team members, 136–40; preservice teachers, recruiting and admitting, 144–47; racial justice commitment, developing, 140–42

questioning case study, 73–75

race: centering, 113; discomfort in discussions of, 116; race-evasive, as term, 187n2; race-evasive ideologies, 70; racial categories, creation of, 189n15; racial conflict, in RJP classes, 121–24; racial hate crimes, children's response to, 48–49; racial hostility, of US schools, 83–85; racial identity, strategic support for, in RJPs,

127–28; racial power dynamics, hiddenness of, 7; racial reframes, Four I's of oppression and advantage, 85–87; in RJPs, explicitness about, 114–18; as social construction, 89–91; teachers' incomplete understandings of, 9. See also racism; *entries beginning "racial"*

racial affinity spaces (identity caucusing), 157–58

racial hierarchies: All Things Being Equal tool and, 39; as basis for social order in United States, 6; influence of, 4; institutional racism and, 99; scientific racism and, 90; in slavery role-playing "games," 57; White Out tool as maintaining, 27

racial ideology and curriculum, 63–82; case studies on, overview of, 64–65; default setting, shift to anti-racism, 81–82; introduction to, 21–22, 63–64; openmindedness case study, 70–73; questioning case study, 73–75; transformation case study, 75–81; White protectionism case study, 65–70

racial justice: collective engagement in internal work of, 142–44; developing commitment to, 140–2; racial justice leadership, 136–40; spaces for teacher education advancing, 154–66; in teacher education, 111, 113, 114. See also teacher education, humanizing racial justice in

racial justice programs (RJPs). See *entries beginning "teacher education"; names of specific programs*

racism: environmental racism, 74–75; health effects of, 58–60; as institutional, 99–100; internalized racism, 91; levels of awareness of, 81; outside of the classroom, instances of, 83–84; reverse racism, 66–67; scientific racism, 90; White people's responsibility for ending, 16–17. *See also* curricular Tools of Whiteness; race; Whiteness
Racism Without Racists (Bonilla-Silva), 187n2
racist curriculum: conclusions on, 167–69; curricular tools of Whiteness, 25–62; introduction to, 1–24; racial ideology and curriculum, 63–82; teacher education, disrupting Whiteness in, 109–33; teacher education, humanizing of racial justice in, 135–66; teacher education, reframing understandings of race within, 83–108. *See also* #Curriculum-SoWhite; *detailed entries for these concepts*
Racist Reproduction tool, 54–57
radical care, 149
Radical Healing Workshops, 154–55
Radical Possibilities, 23, 166
Reading Horizons, 49–50
reframes, 85–107; ideological racial reframes, 87–91; institutional racial reframes, 98–103; internalized racial reframes, 92–98; interpersonal racial reframes, 103–7; racial reframes and the Four I's of oppression and advantage, 85–87

Reign, April, 2
relationships holding emotions (in RJPs), 147–53
resistance (to change), 80, 115–16, 119–20, 130, 151
respectability politics, 190–91n1
restorative circles, 123
Rethinking Schools, 42
reverse racism, 66
Rich, Cynthia W., 37–38
Rivera-McCutchen, Rosa, 149
RJPs (racial justice programs). See *entries beginning "teacher education"; names of specific programs*
Robinson, Jennifer, 126
role-playing, Racist Reproduction tool and, 54–57
Rosemond, Ebony, 54

Saad, Layla F., 7
Santos, Carlos E., 38–9
Santos, Kimberly R., 137
S-Aungkh, Aqkhira, 52, 53
saviorism, 8, 17, 97
Sawyer, Margaret, 54
Scholastic (publisher), 35–37
schools: questioning White cultural norms in, 106–7; racial hostility of, 83–86; racial hostility of US schools, 83–85; school curricula, toxicity of, 3; White cultural norms in, questioning of, 106–7
Sealey-Ruiz, Yolanda, 13
Secret, Carrie, 15
self, questioning of, 15–16
settler colonialism, 10, 32–33
Shalaby, Carla, 20
Singleton, Glenn, 94
slavery. See enslavement
#SlaveryWithASmile, 35

slow violence, 58–60
social order, in United States, 6–8
Southern Poverty Law Center, 57
spaces for teacher education
    advancing racial justice,
    154–66; community engage-
    ment, 161–63; introduction to,
    154–55; one-on-one meet-
    ings, 159–61; organization of
    students into cohorts, 155–57;
    post-graduation teacher sup-
    port, 163–66; racial affinity
    spaces, 157–58
Stamped from the Beginning
    (Kendi), 9
Steinberg, Shirley R., 7
strategies of Whiteness, authentic
    emotions versus, 149–52
students (in RJPs): organization
    into cohorts, 155–57; resis-
    tance, explicitness in address-
    ing, 119–20; Whiteness,
    ensuring disruption of, 125–32.
    See also *entries beginning
    "teacher education"*
students of Color (in RJPs): racial
    affinity groups and, 158; racial
    conflicts and, 122–24; recruit-
    ing, 144–47; 360 support and,
    127; Whiteness from, 121
systemic racism, problem of, 2.
    See also Four I's of oppression
    and advantage

Tatum, Beverly Daniel, 81–82
Taylor, Sonya Renee, 18
Teacher Activist Groups, 166
teacher education, disrupt-
    ing Whiteness in, 109–33;
    explicitness about race, in
    RJPs, 114–18; introduction to,
    22–23, 109–12; race, centering

of, 113; RJP classes, disruption
    of Whiteness in, 118–24; RJPs,
    list of, 112; students' White-
    ness, ensuring disruption of,
    125–32
teacher education, humanizing
    racial justice in, 135–66; intro-
    duction to, 22–23, 135–36;
    program teams, 136–47; rela-
    tionships holding emotions,
    147–53; spaces for teacher
    education advancing racial
    justice, 154–66
teacher education, reframing
    understandings of race within,
    83–108; conclusions on, 108;
    ideological racial reframes,
    87–91; institutional racial
    reframes, 98–103; internal-
    ized racial reframes, 92–98;
    interpersonal racial reframes,
    103–7; introduction to, 3;
    racial reframes and the Four I's
    of oppression and advantage,
    85–87; US schools, racial
    hostility of, 83–85
teachers: incomplete understand-
    ings of race, 9; socialization of,
    5–6; teacher education as locus
    for disruption of racial ideology
    of, 13–14, 62; teacher objectiv-
    ity, assigning blame and, 42;
    Tools of Whiteness and, 26;
    White teachers, as perpetra-
    tors of viral racist curriculum,
    4. *See also* racial ideology and
    curriculum; *entries beginning
    "teacher education"*
textbooks: Atlantic slave trade
    example in, 30–32, 31*f*; chattel
    slavery depictions in, 32–39; as
    curricular Tools of Whiteness,

33–34; Not That Bad tool in, 37
Three-Fifths Compromise, 1
360 support, 126–29
Tools of Whiteness, 22, 26. *See also* curricular Tools of Whiteness
toys, lack of diversity in, 77–78
transformation case study, 75–81
Trump, Donald, 41–42
Tuck, Eve, 32–33

UCLA, Center X, 138–39, 141, 163
The Underground Railroad (Whitehead), 47
Undoing Racism workshop, 80, 89, 95, 189n12, 189n15
United States: colonialism and anti-Blackness in, 10; schools, racial hostility of, 83–85; social order in, 6–8
Urban Education and Social Justice Program (UESJ, University of San Francisco), 154, 157–58
Urban Teacher Education Program (UTEP, University of Chicago), 112, 113, 117–18, 130, 161–62, 164–65

Vega, Blanca, 158
victims, blaming of, 100–2
Villarreal, Christina "V": on accountability to children of Color, 132; on counseling students out of RJPs, 129–30; on crying, 150; on foreshadowing experiences of centering race, 116–17; on hiring, 137; racial affinity groups, work with, 158; on racial identities, 127–28; on

relationships in RJPs, 148; on student breakthroughs, 153
violence, curriculum violence, 57–58
viral racist curriculum, 2–5

Walker, Angie, 46
White awareness, levels of, 81
White children, White Gaze tool and, 47–48
White Gaze tool, 43–49
Whitehead, Colson, 47
Whiteness: BIPOC enactment of, 110; description of, 110; as ideology, 6–7; methods of enacting, 8; non-present imaginary Whiteness, power of, 43; nowhere to hide concept of, 125–32; as part of the curriculum, 120–1; realizing biases of, 97–98; recognizing systemic benefits of, 96–97; as social construction, 94; strategies of, authentic emotions versus, 149–52; White protectionism case study, 65–70; White socialization, 5–10. *See also* curricular tools of Whiteness; teacher education, disrupting Whiteness in
White Out tool, 27–30
White privilege, 19–20, 67, 73–4, 76, 85, 124
White racial identity, 5, 7, 94–96
White Rage (Anderson), 56
White supremacy, 6, 26, 93
White teachers, as perpetrators of viral racist curriculum, 4
White tears, 150
Whooley, Laura, 34–35, 181n18
Wise, Tim, 18
Woodson, Carter G., 58